# BUILDING YOUR PORTFOLIO

## The CILIP guide

# BUILDING YOUR PORTFOLIO

## The CILIP guide

SECOND EDITION

Margaret Watson

facet publishing

© Margaret Watson 2008, 2010

Published by Facet Publishing
7 Ridgmount Street, London WC1E 7AE
www.facetpublishing.co.uk

Facet Publishing is wholly owned by CILIP: the Chartered Institute
of Library and Information Professionals.

*British Library Cataloguing in Publication Data*
A catalogue record for this book is available from the British Library.

ISBN 978-1-85604-714-2

First published 2008
This second edition 2010
Reprinted digitally thereafter

Text printed on FSC accredited material.

**Mixed Sources**
Product group from well-managed
forests and other controlled sources
www.fsc.org Cert no. SA-COC-1565
© 1996 Forest Stewardship Council
FSC

Typeset from author's files in 11/15 pt Aldine 721 and Chantilly by
Facet Publishing Production.
Printed and made in Great Britain by MPG Books Group, UK.

# Contents

# Contributors

## Atiya Afghan

Almost by chance, and on the suggestion of her daughter, Tia became a library assistant at Whitgift School. Within a few months she realized the importance of getting qualified and a year later obtained her NVQ Level 3 in Library and Information Management; six months after that she was awarded the Affiliated Member of CILIP (ACLIP) qualification by the Chartered Institute of Library and Information Professionals (CILIP). She decided to continue studying and in 2009 was awarded her Chartership by CILIP. She is currently Head Librarian at Whitgift School.

## Alan Brine

Alan is Head of Technical Services at De Montfort University Library, where he runs a team of IT professionals who maintain the library network and associated systems and provide support and training for the staff and students. Previously to this he was the Manager for Information Science at the Learning and Teaching Support Network Centre for Information and Computer Sciences at Loughborough University. He is currently studying for a doctorate at Loughborough University. He has presented a number of papers on his research at international conferences, including the International Federation of Library Associations and Institutions (IFLA), many of which have been published in the professional press. As a Chartered Member of the Chartered Institute of Library and Information Professionals, he is professionally active in its groups, providing training for its Members and mentoring candidates who are registered with CILIP.

## Margaret Chapman

Margaret started out as a library assistant, gaining her initial Library and Information Science (LIS) qualification through the part-time route while working full-time. From an early start in medical libraries during which she Chartered, Margaret's career progressed through posts in further and higher education where she achieved a Certificate in Education and a Master's in Librarianship, again while working full-time. She became a Chartered Fellow in 2001 and revalidated her Fellowship in 2006. Significant strands in her career have been information skills, para-professional education and staff management – each connected by a commitment to the personal and professional development of individuals. Among her wider professional activities, Margaret served as a member of the CILIP Chartership Board, standing down when she joined the Qualifications and Professional Development (QPD) team of CILIP. After over 40 years in the LIS profession she is now working as a freelance trainer and consultant and continues her involvement in qualifications and professional development.

## Sarah Cockroft

Sarah is Team Leader Operations and Customer Services (East Area), Calderdale Libraries. She started as a library assistant, was then a supervisor within Calderdale libraries and, after gaining further skills and qualifications, is now Team Leader for nine libraries, an art gallery and three mobile libraries. She gained her ACLIP qualification in 2009.

## Roberta Crossley

Roberta has worked for Calderdale Libraries since 1978. In 1987 she undertook the City and Guilds Library and Information Assistants Certificate at Huddersfield Technical College, being tutored by Margaret Chapman. She was quite pleasantly surprised to bump into Margaret some 22 years later in 2009 when undertaking her ACLIP. She is currently Team Leader for Calderdale Libraries West Area.

## Chloe French

After completing an undergraduate degree in English and German Studies at the University of Birmingham Chloe spent a year as a graduate trainee at the Institute of Advanced Legal Studies library. She studied for an MA in Library and Information Studies at University College London and joined West Sussex Library Service as a trainee librarian. She currently works as a librarian at Crawley Library.

## Jim Jackson

Jim has held a number of library posts within the Academic Services Division of the University of Exeter. He is an active member of CILIP's National Committee for Affiliated Members. He was awarded his ACLIP in 2005. He also writes a regular column for *Associates*, the electronic library support staff journal. He is the Web Editor for the Affiliates Group, and was responsible for the introduction of audio files on their website. He has also chaired sessions at recent 'Umbrella' conferences and been a member of the Policy Forum for CILIP. He is a keen advocate for front line staff and for the continued development of the Framework of Qualifications.

## Heather Karpicki

Heather has worked as a library assistant in public libraries, at Area HQ, Travelling Library Supervisor, and as a bibliotherapist before moving into her current role as Team Leader for Central Area, Calderdale Libraries. She enjoys engaging with the community and promoting local studies. She gained her ACLIP qualification in 2009.

## Ayub Khan

Ayub is Head of Libraries (Strategy), Warwickshire County Council. He is a former board member of CILIP's Chartership Board and has served on the joint Accreditation/Chartership regulations working group for the Framework of Qualifications. He has held a number of posts in public libraries specializing in schools', young people's and community librarianship. His most recent role was that of Principal Project Officer at the Library of Birmingham. He is a CILIP Councillor and chairs CILIP's Equal Opportunities and Diversity panel. Ayub is a former Career Development Group (CDG) President. He achieved his Fellowship in 2004.

## Michael Martin

Michael started working in libraries at Middlesex Polytechnic. As it became Middlesex University he qualified and then went on to Charter in 1996. A few years later he went to work as an information manager at The Library Association, later CILIP, and became an adviser for qualifications in 2004. Michael speaks at many Certification and Chartership events. He revalidated his Chartership in June 2007.

## Karen Newton

Karen has had a long and varied career with Sunderland Public Libraries. She is currently Manager at the Washington Library and Customer Service Centre which opened in June 2009. After working on the pilot project for the ACLIP, Karen enrolled on the part-time BSc (Hons) Information Studies course at Northumbria University, which she will complete in 2010. Karen freely admits that she would never have thought of undertaking such a course if CILIP's Certification Scheme had not helped her to realize her capabilities.

## Lesley Randall

Lesley returned to Wandsworth Libraries in 2001 after working for several years in community/arts projects in London and ten years in Arts Management in Brighton. She is passionate about reader development and learning in libraries. She currently works as a senior library assistant in the new Wandsworth Town Library. Lesley was awarded her Membership of the Chartered Institute of Library and Information Professionals (MCLIP) in 2009.

## Shamin Renwick

Shamin is Divisional Librarian (Agriculture and Sciences) at The University of the West Indies, St. Augustine, Trinidad and Tobago, and has presented conference papers, workshops and posters. Shamin has written several refereed publications as well as having co-edited the books *Caribbean Libraries in the 21st Century* (2007) and *Directory of Caribbean Agricultural Information Sources* (2009). She is the recipient of several awards including the Chartered Fellowship of CILIP (FCLIP), received at CILIP Umbrella Conference 2007.

## Paul Tovell

Paul has been a librarian in Nottinghamshire public libraries for four years. He shares responsibility for selecting and managing resources for all county libraries, contributes to reader development work, and mentors colleagues through Chartership and Certification. He is secretary of the East Midlands Career Development Group, which supports people in obtaining professional qualifications and managing their careers.

## Keith Trickey

Keith lectures part-time at Liverpool Business School, delivers training in cataloguing and classification and personal development and has coached and mentored for more than 15 years. He is also passionate about well-being, diet, cycling and family history. He is currently engaged in research on Library of Congress subject headings.

## Margaret Watson

Margaret Watson was President of CILIP 2003–4; the main theme for her presidency was continuing professional development (CPD). She chaired CILIP's Qualifications Framework Steering Group, and is currently Chair of CILIP's Ethics Panel, a member of the Encompass Steering Group and CILIP's representative on the UK Inter-Professional Group (UKIPG). Margaret started in academic libraries before moving to lecturing in 1987, becoming Head of Subject Division and acting Head of Department at Northumbria University. She was a member of the Northern Training Group, based in the North East, for many years and was involved in advanced ICT training for public librarians. Now retired, Margaret works as a consultant and has facilitated training for CILIP Assessment Panels and the CILIP Mentor Scheme.

## Sue Westcott

Sue is Head of ICT Services at Communities and Local Government and Vice Chair of the CILIP Government Library and Information Group. She has worked in four government departments in a variety of knowledge management roles. She is a CILIP mentor and was a CILIP councillor and member of the CILIP Executive Board. She is a member of Information Matters Task and Finish Group. Sue was awarded her FCLIP in 2004.

## Ruth Wilkinson

Ruth spent the first 12 years of her career in the hotel and catering industry. After running her own business for five years she decided to have a go at something else and graduated from Northumbria University in 2004 with a first class BSc (Hons) in Information and Communication Management. Her first post was as Assistant Librarian for a law firm based in Newcastle. In January 2005 she was appointed Information Specialist at National Building Specifications (NBS), and in October 2007 was promoted to Information Services Co-coordinator. Her role involves managing the content of online information products that serve the construction industry.

## Keith Wilson

Keith is Technical Information Director for RIBA Enterprises Ltd. Before moving to RIBA Enterprises he worked for Faulkner Brown, a firm of architects, and was awarded honorary membership of RIBA in recognition of his contribution to that profession. Keith started his professional career with Northumberland County Library. He is Chair of the Chartership Board and a qualified trainer. He is also a CILIP mentor and Chair of the Employer Liaison Group, School of Computing, Engineering and Information Sciences at Northumbria University. He was awarded his FCLIP in 2007.

# Foreword

Presenting evidence to the professional body has always been a necessity for the information professionals determined to enhance their skills and develop themselves, and also for the service they provide to their clientele. The format for the presentation of that evidence has differed over the years but the need to be able to present materials cogently to prove a level of competence that would mean something to other professionals has always been central to the library and information profession. Recent years have seen the portfolio become the vehicle of choice to present one's professional development. Certification, Chartership, Fellowship and Revalidation with the professional body require the submission of a portfolio as a means of presenting one's professional competence. This is not because it is the latest 'fad' but because it is a way to build a framework that becomes a foundation for professional practice.

Creating a portfolio for most individuals appears at first to be a daunting task. The effort required should not be underestimated; however, the benefits that the individual receives from undertaking the process are great. The portfolio is more than just a tool for recording one's progress; it enables one to plan one's development by analysing the journey taken so far in one's career. It is a tool for personal development planning, concerned with current or future job roles, and should include additional activities that the individual undertakes outside the work-based environment.

As is the case with all journeys of discovery that lead to achievement and recognition, the process is enhanced with the help of a guide. A mentor can be a pillar of support, being able to suggest useful contacts and sources that will be of benefit to the individual, along with other important forms of guidance. The experience of a mentor can be an important component for the successful candidate. However, the mentor can only help with the decisions that must be made. If an individual has the guidance of a mentor, although they will benefit from this support, which is considerable, they must still select appropriate structures and methods that suit their style of learning and way of working.

One of the most important aspects of developing a portfolio is that it introduces the individual to the concept of *reflective practice*; consequently no book on building portfolios can be without a chapter on reflective practice. Simply placing certificates or statements into a portfolio merely creates a list of things that have been done; it does not enable one to get the maximum from one's experiences. To do this one must review what they have done on each occasion and then record their thoughts regarding the event. This provides the opportunity to:

- think about one's experiences
- observe and review activities to determine any lessons to be learned
- assimilate one's experiences and think before taking any action
- perform research to form one's own view
- analyse one's experience
- exchange experiences with others at appropriate times.

Reflective practice, for most individuals, is not their natural way of learning. Most people need to learn how to be reflective and develop the requisite skills that will allow them to achieve this. Building a portfolio helps the individual to develop reflective practice to the point where it becomes an acquired skill that can be applied when required. Reflection should take place in both the short term and the longer term. One's thoughts immediately after a training event may differ from what they are six months down the line, when other experiences may have caused one to rethink training received at an earlier stage.

Using a portfolio to maintain a record of achievements enables one to reflect upon experiences and plot a development path for skills that will also help in planning out one's career. Reflective practice provides the tools for self-evaluation to review and develop a career path. Other learning styles, including activist theoretical and pragmatic (Honey and Mumford, 1986), exist and individuals should be aware of their own personal learning style so that they can use this to their advantage when seeking development opportunities. Training that suits an individual's learning style will increase the benefit that they will receive from the training. Reflection upon training will ensure that the maximum benefit is gained before committing it to record within the portfolio.

Building a curriculum vitae (CV) as part of the portfolio process helps each person create a record of achievements. This supports the process of applying for future employment. Creating a portfolio provides the foundations of any application or CV for any position that has been advertised. An appropriately structured portfolio will enable easier extraction of the information needed to fill in a job application, by simply measuring the skills required for a post against those that have been clearly recorded in the portfolio.

The portfolio is a written record of the skills acquired over the period that one has been building the portfolio. In the library and information profession the range of skills acquired by professionals can be extremely broad and may include aspects of building management, finance, personnel management, computing and teaching, as well as some of the more traditional skills such as cataloguing and information retrieval. This diverse set of skills makes imperative the use of a portfolio by all individuals in order to keep track of one's development in all areas.

Combined with the fact that it is, in addition, a record of achievements, a portfolio enables one to look at a specification for a job and compare one's skills against it to determine whether one's skill set is appropriate for the job on offer. Possibly the most important aspect of building a portfolio is not the fact that it can lead to becoming a Chartered Member of the professional body, but that one can monitor the development of one's skills and analyse progress, enabling one to take the next step on one's professional journey.

Individuals should regularly analyse their skills through a SWOT (strengths, weaknesses, opportunities and threats) analysis as described by Boydell and Leary (1986). This provides a foundation for professional development, so that one can effectively ascertain which skills one is sufficiently well trained in and which skills would benefit from being developed. An advantage of recording one's development in a portfolio is that it supports this process by making the task of performing a training needs analysis much easier. To analyse one's training needs one should first audit one's skills, as suggested by Williamson (1986), and then determine which skills still require developing. A portfolio, by recording the acquisition and development of skills, gives the individual a ready tool with which to check their skill set.

A portfolio is used as a key part of personal development planning and the skills development cycle. Jackson (2001) describes the process as:

- planning
- doing
- recording
- reviewing
- evaluating.

When building a portfolio, a personal development plan (PDP) is required, and following these steps will ensure that individuals reflect on their experience and get the most from their training and development. Experience, gained from those who have used portfolios in library and information science, has shown that building a portfolio can lead to individuals having an increased ability in understanding their own development and keeping a record of it (Brine and Feather, 2003). Consequently, using a portfolio will lead to library and information professionals having a better grasp of their development, leading to a better prepared workforce for the sector.

Individuals should start a portfolio as soon as is practically possible in their career because the material generated through training and development can soon accumulate and become difficult to manage. There are many aspects to building a portfolio, and among those that require serious consideration from the outset are:

- what to include
- how to annotate
- how to structure
- ways to index.

Specific suggestions in these areas, including tools to use, are available to support individuals (Brine, 2005). The most important thing to note, however, is that the individual takes full control and ownership of the process. One must decide for oneself what is appropriate. Some aspects of the portfolio, such as the personal statement, will be guided by the individual's experience and use of techniques developed during the creation of the portfolio. Additionally, one must be organized, allocating sufficient time to planning how one can obtain the most benefit from one's portfolio and consequently enhance one's continuing professional development.

Building a portfolio can be a daunting task and candidates for professional qualifications must put in a considerable amount of work if they are to create an acceptable one. It is for the individual to develop their own structure and methods to form a framework for their continuing professional development. However, the benefits are many and will support the individual through career development. The chapters that follow provide support, guidance and ideas that the individual can use to formulate their portfolio development. There are no right or wrong answers, but the portfolio must achieve the required level of professional competence and quality. The following chapters will do much to help guide the individual in making choices for meeting the requirements for CILIP qualifications and for personal and career development using the portfolio.

Alan Brine

Head of Technical Services, De Montfort University Library

# Acknowledgements

I should like to thank all the colleagues who have contributed their personal stories for this book, my friends in the Qualifications and Professional Development team at CILIP, the marvellous team of mentors and all the people I have spoken to about CILIP qualifications at various events around the country. Much of the book has been written as a result of those conversations; much of the interest and value is in the personal stories, but any errors are mine. Thanks also to the team at Facet for their help, to Margaret Chapman for her help with the revision and most of all thanks to Charlie for listening and giving me the space to write.

Margaret Watson

# 1

# Introduction

## Purpose of the book

The Chartered Institute of Library and Information Professionals (CILIP) introduced its new Framework of Qualifications in April 2005. There are four elements in the scheme: Certification, Chartered Membership, Fellowship and Revalidation for Chartered Members and Fellows. The assessment of each level of qualification is by submission of a portfolio. This book has been written to support any Member of CILIP who wishes to apply for a professional qualification. This revised edition reflects the changes to Certification and contains some new personal contributions. For many of us working in the library and information profession the production of a portfolio was a new experience and there has been much discussion about the nature of the portfolio. This book is designed to answer some of those questions, sharing the experience, hints and tips of putting a portfolio together from colleagues who have successfully gained their qualifications.

Each chapter deals with a specific aspect of the portfolio, giving examples from each qualification as appropriate. The book can be either read straight through by potential candidates or used with greater discretion by applicants who may be having difficulties with particular elements of the portfolio.

Alan Brine, in the Foreword, provided an overview of how portfolios can be used in all aspects of a career and how important reflection is for the information professional. Chapter 1 is the introductory chapter, looking at the purpose of the book and briefly outlining CILIP's Framework of Qualifications and the reasons for adopting a portfolio approach. It also discusses the support available to Members as they put together their portfolios, especially the CILIP Mentor Scheme. There are two very important aspects to the Framework: all portfolios must meet specified assessment criteria and applicants must demonstrate an appropriate level of reflective writing within their portfolios. Chapter 2 discusses the assessment criteria and attempts to show how you can build your portfolio to ensure that it meets those criteria; Keith Wilson, Chair of the Chartership Board, gives the views of an assessor and moderator. Chapter 3 is concerned with reflective writing and how you can begin the habit of reflection and learn to be more evaluative; Keith Trickey talks about his life experience as a reflective writer. Chapters 4 to 7 consider each element of the portfolio in more detail: the CV, the development plan, the personal statement and supporting evidence. Each chapter provides hints and tips about the element it covers and provides personal stories focusing on the element from ACLIPs, MCLIPs, FCLIPs and Members who have revalidated. In the final chapter, Chapter 8, presentation and submission are outlined and some thought is given to what happens next.

All of the chapters in this book refer back to CILIP's website and the information and supporting documentation that can be found there. It is recommended that you check there for the most up-to-date information and formal documentation.

Remember, you are not alone in going through this process; we can learn so much from other people's experiences.

## CILIP's Framework of Qualifications

CILIP's professional qualifications are only available to Members of the Institute. They are the only professional qualifications in library and information work in the UK and are recognized globally.

## Certification scheme

'Certification is the recognition of the contribution made in library and information work by para-professionals' (CILIP website). Applicants must have been working in library and information work for two years (full-time equivalent) or longer. The post-nominals ACLIP are awarded to successful candidates.

A Certified Affiliate with a minimum of two years' relevant post-Certification experience and development can submit an application for Chartership.

## Chartered Membership

'Chartered Membership is the second level of professional qualification awarded by CILIP and is considered the "gold standard" for library and information professionals' (CILIP website). There are various pathways to Chartered Membership, but all Members must submit a portfolio to meet the same assessment criteria. Advice on the most appropriate pathway is available from the QPD team at CILIP.

## Fellowship

'Fellowship is the highest level of professional qualification awarded by CILIP and recognizes a high level of personal commitment and achievement' (CILIP website). Fellowship is normally awarded only to Members who have been on the Register for at least six years, although exceptions may be made in some cases. The new Framework of Qualifications introduced a new category of eligibility for Fellowship for Chartered Members who have successfully completed two cycles of revalidation (see CILIP website).

## Revalidation

'Revalidation is open to all Chartered Members, including Fellows, who wish to gain evidence and recognition of their commitment to personal professional development' (CILIP website). Normally Members complete three years of Revalidation and each year is recognized by CILIP; for some Members who have undergone several years of CPD after Chartership or Fellowship, the submission can be made immediately. A certificate is awarded on successful completion of each three-year cycle of Revalidation (see CILIP website). Currently Revalidation is voluntary, but, in line with other professional associations, CILIP is developing a compulsory CPD Scheme to replace it. Although this scheme may be 'lighter touch' than the current one, it will nevertheless require reflection on personal and professional development through a range of CPD activities.

## The portfolio approach

Building a portfolio to demonstrate your best work is not a new concept. Artists, photographers and architects have always used this approach and recently more professions, such as the teaching profession, have adopted the portfolio concept. Your portfolio is an evaluative review of professional development and should present evidence to demonstrate that you meet the criteria of assessment for the award of a CILIP professional qualification. CILIP sets the criteria (see Chapter 2) and each individual applicant selects their own evidence to meet those criteria. CILIP chose the portfolio approach based on the experience of the Chartership Board, CILIP's equivalent of an examination board, over many years and on the increasing need of information professionals to evaluate, articulate and demonstrate their own effectiveness and value. If we learn early in our careers to analyse, record and evaluate our professional development then it is easier to plan and implement continuous professional development. (Chapter 3 discusses reflective writing in more detail.)

The portfolio approach allows individuals to present information that they have selected to meet the criteria. The evidence should reflect on all professional activities undertaken and provide a rounded picture of each applicant. The emphasis is clearly focused on the individual and what they personally have learned: on output rather than input. The heart of the portfolio is not the posts you have held or the courses you have undertaken but the outcome of those activities. The focus is on you and how you have developed professionally, and personally, to meet the challenges of a demanding and ever-changing information environment. The portfolio covers past achievements, present experience and proposed development.

## Support for portfolio building

For many of us, compiling a portfolio is a new experience so, as well as the handbooks and regulations for each award, there are additional sources of support for candidates. CILIP's Career Development Group (CDG) organizes events specifically for candidates and has regional Candidate Support Officers (CSOs). Much of the support is aimed at Certification and Chartership candidates, but CDG also organizes some events for Fellowship and Revalidation candidates. There are also special courses for those wishing to move from ACLIP to MCLIP. Information on these events is available on the CILIP website: www.cilip.org.uk/jobs-careers/qualifications/cilip-qualifications/portfolio/pages/example.aspx.

Information on becoming a mentor and details of training courses run by CILIP's Personnel, Training and Education Group (PTEG) are also available on the website at www.cilip.org.uk/jobs-careers/qualifications/cilip-qualifications/mentor-scheme/pages/resources.aspx.

The Qualifications and Professional Development (QPD) Department at CILIP can help with individual queries. It also advises overseas candidates on all aspects of their applications.

There are also discussion lists for each qualification, except Fellowship:

Certification: LIS-CILIP-ACLIP
Chartership: LIS-CILIP-REG
Revalidation: LIS-CILIP-REVAL.

To join any of these discussions lists go to www.jiscmail.ac.uk. These lists allow for frank and down-to-earth discussion between candidates.

Another invaluable means of support is the CILIP Mentor Scheme; see www.cilip.org.uk/jobs-careers/qualifications/cilip-qualifications/mentor-scheme/pages/default.aspx.

It is compulsory for all Chartership candidates to have a mentor. It is strongly recommended that all Certification candidates also find one. A list of mentors is available on the CILIP website. You can choose someone from your own sector or someone from a different one. Mentors can operate face-to-face or in a virtual relationship. Mentor support is crucial for overseas Members. Candidates for Fellowship and Revalidation often find it useful to work with a 'buddy' or in a small support group. You can discuss the various elements of your portfolio and use your 'buddy' or support group to check that you have provided relevant and appropriate evidence. A mentor who is registered on the CILIP Mentor Scheme will have undertaken mentor training and will be familiar with the process of building a portfolio. The mentor is not a supervisor but is there to help and support you to select evidence and build the most effective portfolio.

There are also examples of successful portfolios on the CILIP website and held by the Candidate Support Officers in the regions and home nations; but remember, your portfolio is unique – it is about you and how you meet the assessment criteria. There is no perfect model portfolio, just an effective portfolio demonstrating your development.

# 2

## Assessment criteria

### What are assessment criteria?

'All assessment is, at its simplest, the process of judging evidence of achievement' (Herzog, 1996). Each CILIP award recognizes the achievement of the applicant. For CILIP qualifications the evidence put forward is the portfolio. Your portfolio is assessed by at least two professional colleagues: for Chartership and Fellowship by members of CILIP's Chartership Board, and for Certification and Revalidation currently by members of the CILIP Assessment Panel. It is very important for each applicant to become familiar with the particular assessment criteria by which their portfolio will be judged.

As a mentor I have often given the advice that you should keep a copy of the criteria next to your PC or on the desk where you are working on your portfolio. It is so easy to get carried away by collecting evidence and filling in all the requisite templates that you can sometimes forget to focus on the criteria. The assessment criteria tell you what you need to do. To also help ensure you are meeting the criteria, it is advisable to download the appropriate assessment form for your qualification and read it carefully. This is the form that the assessors will use. Ask yourself whether your portfolio presents the correct evidence to meet the criteria.

In this chapter I will discuss the assessment criteria for each award and this will be followed by reflections on assessment by Keith Wilson, Chair of CILIP's Chartership Board. (There are further guidelines for each element of your portfolio in the succeeding chapters.)

## Certification (ACLIP)

To apply for Certification you need to have been working in library and information work for two years (full-time equivalent) and be a Member of CILIP; there are two categories of CILIP Membership – Affiliate and Associate – from which you will need to decide which is most appropriate for you. The category you choose is dependent on the amount of experience you have and the level of responsibility you hold in your current role. Most candidates for Certification will be Affiliate Members but some will be Associate. To find out which category of Membership is right for you go to www.cilip.org.uk/membership/whocanjoin.aspx.

The criteria for assessment for Certification are:

1   An ability to evaluate personal performance and service performance.
2   An understanding of the ways in which your personal, technical and professional skills have developed through training and developmental activities and/or through practice.
3   An appreciation of the role of library and information services in the wider community.

All forms, templates and associated guidance notes plus examples of successful applications can be found at www.cilip.org.uk/jobs-careers/qualifications/cilip-qualifications/certification/Pages/default.aspx.

## Evaluating personal and service performance

The first criterion is looking for your ability to evaluate your own performance and that of the service where you are employed.

Evaluating personal performance (criterion 1a) means that you need to present evidence of your own learning and contribution and think about its effectiveness. In other words, don't just describe what you have done – try to explain what you learned from your various experiences and how you can apply that knowledge in the future, or what specific impacts your contributions have already made on the service (see Chapter 3, 'Reflective writing'). For example, you may have attended a course on marketing and been able to make a contribution to putting on an event in the library, or you may have suggested a different procedure for dealing with newly returned books. You should reflect on how your personal performance has changed over the last 12 to 24 months and where improvements still need to be made.

When you evaluate the service (criterion 1b), you need to understand the aims of the service and how they are or are not currently met. If any user surveys have been carried out, you can comment on those. Pick out any areas which have improved since the survey, and give your own thoughts on the improvements. Another possible example could be that you have visited another library and been impressed by what you saw; you may then have suggested a change in your own workplace and can record whether this went well. All these points should be mentioned in the personal statement template and, where appropriate, evidence given in the supporting documentation.

## Understanding the ways in which personal, technical and professional skills have developed through training and developmental activities and/or through practice

The second criterion relates to your personal and professional development; it relates to an understanding of how enhancing your skills and knowledge improves your performance and that of the service. You should use the personal development plan (PDP) to show how you have analysed your development needs and, importantly, what you are going to do about them (see Chapter 5, 'Professional development plans'). Your CV can show any training you have attended and any development achieved through work experience. Again, you can give any evidence of training or development activities in the supporting documentation. Don't forget to evaluate the training you have been on and show how this has impacted on you and/or on your service. You should use your personal statement to record the outcomes of this personal and professional development.

## Appreciation of the role of library/information services in the wider community

The third criterion can be met by showing how aware you are of how your role, or how the service in which you work, interacts with (or fits) within your user community. You will need to understand the mission (or aims and objectives) of your service. You could also look at how your service might complement the other services available in your area. In the guidance notes the wider community can be interpreted as:

- the library/information service
- the employing organization
- the users and potential users
- the area in which the service operates
- other library/information services within the area
- the sector in which the service operates
- partners in any collaborative projects
- any other community as appropriate.

If you are working in an information unit you will need to show that you understand the business plan of the organization. If you are working in a school library you will need to show how your library service supports the child in his/her learning. You can use the personal statement to demonstrate this, as well as any appropriate supporting evidence. You can also show how widely read you are about the information profession or how active you are in the profession in your PDP.

## Chartership (MCLIP)

Whichever pathway you have taken to Chartership, through ACLIP, work experience and first degree or through an approved Master's course, all applicants must provide evidence that they meet identical criteria. Your portfolio should demonstrate that you have:

- an ability to reflect critically on personal performance and to evaluate service performance

- an active commitment to continuing professional development
- an ability to analyse personal and professional development and progression with reference to experiential and developmental activities
- a breadth of professional knowledge and understanding of the wider professional context.

## Reflection on performance and professional development

The first and third criteria are really all about being a reflective practitioner, thinking about what you have done in the workplace since Certification or following your educational qualification. Your CV will provide the factual information on posts you have held, courses you have attended and development activities you have undertaken, so the personal evaluative statement should be reflective – what all this has meant for you and your information service. Through your registration period you must maintain a record of any activity which helps you develop as an information practitioner. Evaluate the activity and then look back and review what has happened since you first recorded the development. Sometimes it takes several weeks before the full benefit of any training or development can begin to be felt.

## Commitment to continuing professional development

The personal professional development plan (PPDP) should show your active commitment to continuing professional development, as well as any additional lists of training and development activities (see Chapter 5).

## Breadth of professional development

The final criterion should be evidenced in your personal evaluative statement, the reading that you do for professional development and the supporting documentation. You should be able to demonstrate that you have a good awareness of the body of professional knowledge (www.cilip.org.uk/jobs-careers/qualifications/accreditation/bpk/Pages/default.aspx) and that you understand how it operates in the workplace.

## Fellowship (FCLIP)

'The criteria for the award of Fellowship are defined in terms of the enhancement of your intellectual and professional skills and the contribution you have made to the development of the profession' (Fellowship handbook). The portfolio for Fellowship should contain evidence of:

- substantial achievement in professional practice
- significant contribution to all or part of the profession
- active commitment to continuing professional development.

The three key words are 'substantial', 'significant' and 'active'. The portfolio should present evidence which demonstrates your knowledge and skills, enhanced by experience and professional development, and what impact that knowledge and those skills have made on the profession. Every submission at Fellowship level will be very different, as experienced practitioners will come from a wide range of sectors, with varying degrees of specialism. Your portfolio should contain a great deal of analysis and reflection on your career to date. Perhaps even more than with the other qualifications, the importance of reflective writing must be emphasized here. Your portfolio must be much more than a description of your career. Each applicant will choose their own themes on which to focus the portfolio, but the evidence must meet those general criteria.

## Revalidation

Revalidation is currently available for Chartered Members and Fellows and provides a formal way to record your continuing professional development. Most regulated professions in the UK have compulsory revalidation in response to the dynamic changes that are facing all professionals in the workplace. Many information professionals follow CPD programmes to enhance their knowledge, skills and expertise, and CILIP is seeking to record that achievement. All candidates must demonstrate the following:

- critical evaluation of personal learning outcomes from a range of training and development activities
- increased competence in a range of professional and management skills developed through professional practice
- evidence of continuous professional development through reading, participation in professional affairs, and contribution to, or attendance at, courses/conferences, etc.

The first criterion is once again about being a reflective practitioner; think about what you have done and what impact training and development has had on you and your work. The second focuses on your work experience and how you have gained further or different expertise over the qualifying time. The final criterion focuses on CPD other than training, and looks at a range of activities which will have contributed to your growth as an information professional. Many information professionals will already be required to carry out this sort of analysis and evaluation of themselves as part of performance review or appraisal.

## Assessment

The assessment of CILIP qualifications is currently carried out by the Chartership Board and the CILIP Assessment Panel (CAP). The Chartership Board assesses Chartership and Fellowship candidates; the CAP assesses Certification and Revalidation candidates. Dates of Board and CAP meetings can be found on the CILIP website.

## CILIP Chartership Board

The Chartership Board is made up of volunteers from a range of sectors who are senior information professionals. They meet five times a year to discuss Chartership and Fellowship applications. Each portfolio is normally assessed by two Board members and then, in the case of rejection, by an all-panel assessment. CILIP appoints two external examiners to monitor the work of the Board (www.cilip.org.uk/jobs-careers/qualifications/cilip-qualifications/chartership-board/Pages/Chartershipboard.aspx).

## CILIP Assessment Panel (CAP)

The CAP works in a similar way to the Chartership Board and is made up of volunteers who are MCLIPs and who have been trained by CILIP as assessors. Many CAP members also have experience as assessors with national vocational qualifications (NVQs) or in further/higher education. Each portfolio is sent to two members of the CAP; if there is disagreement, a third member will be asked to look at the portfolio as well. All-panel assessments are carried out if necessary.

### Hints and tips

☞ Read the criteria carefully at the beginning of the process.

☞ Keep a copy of the assessment criteria on your desk or at the front of your portfolio file.

☞ Download a copy of the assessment form for the appropriate qualification and use it as a checklist before you submit.

☞ Make sure that the evidence in your portfolio demonstrates how you meet the criteria.

☞ Give your portfolio to a mentor or critical friend to proofread and check against the criteria.

☞ The assessors can only assess what is put before them, so make sure that your portfolio includes all necessary elements and meets the assessment criteria.

CASE STUDY 2.1
## Keith Wilson: The criteria of assessment – why have them?

CILIP's four routes to recognition of personal professional achievement provide a flexible framework for library and information service workers to extend and modernize their knowledge and skills, and for this progression to be recognized in formal professional qualifications. Central to this process is the submission from the applicant of evidence for assessment, making the case for qualification. The process involves a number of professional and administrative colleagues and is open to independent scrutiny. Assessment of applications needs to be rigorous, fair, transparent and supportive.

A standardized question-and-answer examination is inappropriate for many reasons, including inability to accommodate the increasing diversity of work that CILIP Members do; differences in the evidence applicants would prefer to use to make a case; development of the evidence-based profession; and opportunity to emphasize information that applicants feel will reinforce their case. Question-and-answer examinations concentrate on outputs. The portfolio solves these issues, and enables standards to be maintained and the Framework of Qualifications to be developed through experience and changing circumstance.

How do applicants know what is expected? How do applicants and assessors know what is and is not acceptable? How do those outside of the profession judge the value of qualified Members? Standards for evaluation provide the answer, known as the criteria of assessment. These have nothing to do with making sure that applicants submit the right paperwork (although this is important); they indicate what needs to be done to ensure that an application is acceptable, and they help to achieve thoroughness, consistency and fairness. They are concerned with outcome, the personal professional progression that makes and will make a difference in the applicant's workplace, to the wider community and to themselves. They also provide the means by which others can judge the value of CILIP qualifications. How do the criteria affect those involved in the process?

## Applicants and assessment criteria

Although emphasis and expectations differ according to what qualifications applicants are applying for, three broad objectives form the backbone to the criteria for the four routes:

1   Ability to critically evaluate is the first objective. This goes hand in glove with the ability to reflect on professional experience and knowledge, constantly reassessing need and opportunity in the light of the organization and the changing world in which it and applicants work. This objective provides applicants with the means to demonstrate professional judgement, maturity, knowledge and expertise.
2   The second objective deals with understanding the importance of being up to date with professional development and practice and demonstrating practical application. This enables applicants to show how they are equipped to deal with change, sharing and implementing practice from, and dealing with, issues of concern to the wider profession.
3   The third objective covers reflection on personal performance. Applicants can make the case here for the extent to which they have fused ability, skills and knowledge, demonstrating how they have changed, and what difference they expect this will make in their future career and to their contribution to the profession at large.

These objectives overlay CILIP's body of professional knowledge. Applicants must meet all criteria for their chosen qualification route. An application will not be accepted if one criterion is not met.

## The Chartership Board and assessment criteria

The Chartership Board judges only what is presented by the applicant. Although there is an expectation that applicants will have carefully proofread their applications, and that they are well organized, these aspects are not included in the criteria of assessment. Specified word counts and types of evidence are, however. If assessors are made aware of issues such as nationality, first language or disability, these are taken into account as they may shape the approach the candidate has taken in presenting evidence. Assessment is then made against the criteria of assessment set out in the qualification handbooks.

Assessors will look for objectivity, understanding of role and contribution in the workplace, attention to professional development and demonstration of its value, synthesis of knowledge and experience, and an indication of how all may change/develop in future. Often when mapping evidence to the criteria they will ask 'So what?' or 'Why?' If the answer is not clear there will be a weakness in the application. Where there is weakness or omission, the assessors may ask the applicant to supply additional information or attend a short professional interview. They will base their requirements on the criteria, with questions designed to help the applicant review the application against the criteria.

When the Board agrees that an application will be rejected, the reasons are always based on the criteria. An explanation of the decision is always accompanied by supporting guidance from the Board.

Where the assessors offer suggestions to successful applicants for further development, they will be based on the criteria, and may be accompanied also by suggestions for ways in which future portfolios may better meet the requirements.

Experience and expertise is shared within the Board both during the assessment process and generally, and is reflected in regular reviews of procedure. Assessment criteria help to avoid subjective judgements.

## CILIP Assessment Panel and assessment criteria

The CILIP Assessment Panel has the same operational procedures as its parent Chartership Board. Evidence presented, however, is often broader and more diverse than for Chartered Member and Fellow applications, particularly for Revalidation. Applicants' ability to relate the relevance and consequence of evidence to the assessment criteria helps the assessors to identify objectivity and increasing professional maturity.

## External examiners and moderators

The Board's external examiners provide an independent viewpoint and ensure that the Board is thorough, fair and objective. They also help ensure that the criteria for the Open University credit transfer scheme are met. Without the criteria of assessment it would be impossible for the examiners to be confident that standards were being met. The examiners' annual report to CILIP Council is based on the success of the whole assessment process in achieving consistency against the criteria. Within the CAP, moderators appointed from the Chartership Board play an equivalent role to the external examiners, helping to ensure that the process is anchored to the criteria of assessment.

## Mentors

The role of the mentor in helping towards a focused application cannot be overestimated. Support, guidance, confidence-building and encouragement from an experienced mentor can always be seen in successful applications. The mentor provides a bridge between the criteria and the mentee's perceptions, and can be very effective in helping the mentee avoid submitting what amounts to simply a descriptive application, the most common reason for rejection. CILIP mentors' main task is to support applicants in preparing their applications; without the assessment criteria this task would be unstructured and it would be very difficult to identify lasting personal benefits that will result from the partnership.

## Regional assessors

After conducting an interview with an applicant, the assessors are required by the Chartership Board to provide an opinion as to whether the application meets the criteria of assessment. This opinion is considered together with a re-evaluation of the portfolio by the Board, which decides solely on the basis of the criteria being met.

## Candidate Support Officers and assessment criteria

Training courses for all qualifications are run by Candidate Support Officers from the Career Development Group and by the Personnel Training and Education Group (PTEG), and the assessment criteria form a central element of these. All candidates and mentors should therefore understand the importance of meeting the assessment criteria.

## Conclusion

The criteria of assessment are the building blocks of the Framework of Qualifications. They ensure consistent and high standards for CILIP's professional qualifications, and provide the means by which personal and professional skills, knowledge and abilities can be assessed. Criteria enable those judging the value of CILIP professional qualifications to understand the capabilities, capacity and contribution that Certificated and Chartered Members can make to organizations and communities.

# 3

# Reflective writing

## What is reflective writing?

Reflective writing is the formal, or informal, recording of your thoughts. As Andrew Booth says, reflective practice requires that you learn from your practical professional experience (Booth and Brice, 2004). So first we have to learn to reflect on our learning and our professional practice, and then we have to become accustomed to recording that reflection in writing. By recording the reflection we formalize the process and have a record of our development.

## Reflective practice

Those of you who are fans of Harry Potter will remember a wonderful magical object that Albus Dumbledore owned called the pensieve. Professor Dumbledore could place memories into this stone basin and then relive them, taking Harry with him so he could learn from those memories. This is a good example of reflection (Watton, Collings and Moon, n.d.) and underscores the importance of learning from experience. It is not sufficient to just have an experience; you need to reflect on that experience and evaluate it, and then apply that knowledge to another experience or activity. Deep and sustained learning – becoming able to do something you couldn't do before – only comes through experience. Experience on its own, however, is not enough. Experience needs to be reflected on and made sense of to create knowledge, and this knowledge deepened when it is applied in fresh situations (Thomson, 2006).

So before reflective writing comes reflection. As part of your CPD you should try to get into the habit of being reflective – thinking about the task you have just done, the course you have been on, the discussion you have had that day at work, the article you have just read, and so on. Any activity that is part of your work life should be reflected on, and lessons learned. Of course, as Keith Trickey reveals later in this chapter, reflection can also become a part of your personal development as well as your professional development.

## Evaluation

Most of us are familiar with evaluation forms, often handed out at the end of workshops. Distributing evaluation forms at workshops enables the leader to reflect on the success or otherwise of that particular session and plan any improvements for future events. While working in higher education I often felt that our students suffered from evaluation fatigue, as at the end of the academic year they were given typically evaluation forms for each of the individual modules along with the course as a whole. But for the staff they were an important element in planning or revising the course or individual module for the following year. I also used to try to carry out my own evaluation, by recording my feelings about the elements in the course – what went well or what could have been done better. If other colleagues were involved in teaching the module, then they would add their feedback. I also updated my knowledge of the subject. The personal evaluation, colleagues' feedback, student feedback and other evidence (my reading or courses attended) all contributed to the reflection and then, hopefully, the improvement of the module or course.

## The learning cycle

Most writers on reflective practice refer to Kolb's (1986) model of experiential learning. This is normally represented as a learning cycle although I think it should really be seen as a learning spiral:

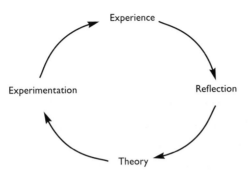

Or simply:

> You do something.
> You think about it.
> You draw conclusions from the experience.
> You plan how you can do it better.
> You do it better.

When I have been asked to speak at CILIP Qualification events or in mentor training sessions I have always joked and said that there is one phrase burned onto my forehead – 'So what?' This is what we should ask ourselves all the time. What have I learned from this activity and what am I going to do as a result? This forms the basis of being a reflective practitioner.

## Reflective writing

Many of us find it quite difficult to write reflectively; like most skills, though, the earlier you start and the more practice you have, the easier it becomes. Andrew Gibbons, whose website (www.andrewgibbons.co.uk) is an invaluable tool for anyone interested in reflective writing, has been keeping a learning log for many years. I attended a talk by Andrew some time ago and saw the huge number of files he had amassed. All of his entries were written by hand and he says that it has now become a way of life for him. He suggests using a template (available for free download on his website) to get started and to not record every little thing, but rather to be selective.

## Keeping a learning log

You can choose to keep a log or diary and complete short entries each day, or perhaps use a weekly diary. Don't just describe or list what happened though. Ask yourself questions (as in the learning cycle above); if possible talk to other people and get their perspective; collect evidence if appropriate.

A colleague of mine used to keep a daybook; in this she would make notes from any meetings or discussions she had been involved in, or from any articles, and so forth, that she had read, and at the end of the week she would record any specific learning outcomes and actions. I was not so organized until I bought myself an A4 Filofax diary; in that I had the list of the day's events but I also made a record, either hand-written or word-processed, of other important thoughts and actions, and a copy of any relevant documents or at least a reference to where those documents were filed. The main problem was that by the end of the academic term it was extremely heavy! But I admit it was very useful to be able to go back and check the record; so much better than trying to rely on memory.

If you keep a diary or logbook you will find that it is so much easier to include reflective writing in your portfolio. For enthusiastic bloggers, why not refine your blogging style and use that as an example of reflective writing?

## Reflective writing for your portfolio

The personal statement in your portfolio is clearly the place where you are required to reflect on your learning and development. You are expected not just to describe what you have done, but to analyse any developmental activity, reflect on the outcomes of that activity and consider how you might apply, or have already applied, what you have learned back in the workplace. So before you write that personal statement you have to reflect. If you have tried to start the process as a reflective practitioner from the time you registered it will be so much easier. Hopefully, you will have kept a learning log or a diary and you will have evidence of development, so it will be relatively straightforward to review your reflections and write your personal statement.

## A daily routine

So how can you start the process? You get into the habit of reviewing any developmental activity and recording your feelings. You can then add a record of discussion with other people and notes from books, reports and articles that you have read on the subject. There are many ways in which you can incorporate reflective writing into your daily routine:

- If you give a presentation, evaluate it; ask colleagues, formally or informally, for their opinions, record how you felt and what you would do differently on another occasion.
- If you go on a visit, record your ideas and note how you could apply anything you saw in your own place of work.
- If you go on a training course, make a note of how useful it was and what skills you were able to apply in the workplace.
- Use the CPD audit sheet on CILIP's website.
- Keep an annotated diary or weekly journal.

It is important to make a record as soon as you can after the event and not to rely on memory. But it is also crucial that you revisit and review that record at a later date, making a note of any subsequent developments or feelings. It sounds a huge task but, as Keith Trickey and Andrew Gibbons both point out, it should become second nature after a while.

This record of self-evaluation and analysis will be a personal record and you are not expected to share it with anyone else, although you may wish to discuss it with your mentor in order to clarify your thoughts.

The record will ultimately provide you with a wonderful source of information for your portfolio. When you come to start compiling, much of the hard work will have been done. You will have a record of your reflection on all aspects of your development and will have significant amounts of supporting evidence, leaving only the task of selecting and organizing the material which best demonstrates that you meet the assessment criteria.

## Hints and tips

☞ At the end of the day/week record any substantial learning or developmental activity.

☞ Discuss the activity with a colleague or mentor and make a note of any interesting points.

☞ Collect any supporting material such as handouts, agendas, flyers, programmes and so forth.

☞ Use the CILIP audit sheet.

☞ Keep any memos, letters or feedback on your performance.

☞ Keep any relevant survey results but add your own notes.

☞ Be honest with yourself.

☞ Set a realistic time aside to reflect.

☞ Use travelling time to record your reflections.

☞ Record your reflections in a diary or make sure that you number the records in some way.

☞ Revisit and review the entries but don't change them; add thoughts if necessary.

CASE STUDY 3.1
### Keith Trickey: Approaches to reflective writing

Sitting down to write is always a very self-conscious act because of the formality involved in presenting our thoughts as text. The conventions of sentence structure and grammar can be ignored in the spoken word, as that huge range of ancillary activity – intonation and gesture – can happily clarify meaning. In text the words themselves have to carry the full weight of the communication, and this is the case whether you work with a pen or a keyboard. So what is the advantage of writing in reflection and how is it best practised?

In briefly reviewing written reflection I will do so from the broad perspective of reflection as a personal development activity, not simply as a required element in professional development. In my own experience professional development is simply one aspect in the complex of activities that keeps an individual moving forward to engage in their life in all its varied aspects. What works in the general case also works, helpfully, in that specific pocket of development named professional development.

## Daily 'mind dump'

The most unstructured form of reflective writing is what Julia Cameron (1997) refers to as 'pages' and involves a regular commitment (for as long as is still proving useful) to produce two or three sides of written A4 each morning (yes, every morning) as a 'mind dump' to allow you to deal with whatever you need to deal with before you start your day. The discipline of sitting each morning to write is really helpful. Sometimes your thoughts sprint out, enabling you to produce sheets of writing in a matter of minutes – your hand struggling to keep up with your racing mind. Sometimes it is 'with painful steps and slow' that the text drags itself out from under the pen; often these sessions provide very helpful information on how you are and what you need to do. The purpose of 'pages' is self-contained. You simply write, and notice as you write what you write (the content) and how you write (emotional element); there is no requirement to move beyond this as the in-process reflection can be carried forward and your mind cleared to allow you to be more effective for the rest of the day.

I used this method for about three years and during that time it proved very useful in giving me insight and clarity about the competing pressures I was dealing with and in enabling me to work more effectively through the day. At the moment I do not do 'pages'. When I need to I will start again – and stop again when they have served their purpose.

## Focused writing

A different approach to reflective writing is offered by Joyce Chapman (1991). Her approach pushes the reflective element more to the fore.

Initially there is the requirement to write about something specific in whatever way is appropriate. You could write a series of well articulated lucid paragraphs, a short poem, or a series of anguished bullet points – all in CAPITAL LETTERS to show your passion! The style you adopt should mirror the task you are undertaking. If it is about your relationship with somebody else, it may be helpful to write it as a dialogue, allowing you to explore the other person's voice. Having completed your writing you then leave a space, because you will be coming back to it later. After a couple of days you re-read the passage and then write a feedback statement to yourself. In reading what you have written you take the role of a supportive friend, and it is with that view that you write the feedback, giving a different perspective on the initial writing. I enjoyed this approach to reflective writing as it allows you to move into the mentor role and be self-nurturing, as opposed to being your most powerful critic.

## 'Three Whats'

If you need to deal with an incident or issue quickly and get some broader thinking around it, then the 'Three Whats?' (Rolfe, Freshwater and Jasper, 2001) is a helpful tool to use. There are three basic components to the approach and these are the three questions What? So What? and Now What? The first What is basically a statement of what has happened. This is followed by So What? Here the significance of the incident is worked out in terms of where it fits in the larger picture of your development. For example, the What – perhaps asking permission to attend a professional development event without having to take leave – may not sound earth shattering, but in the context of So What? it may be the first time that you have asked your organization to support you in this way – having previously taken leave when attending such events. Now that indicates a significant shift in self-valuing in the workplace and it is important that you notice it. Now you can move on to Now What? This gives the action-centred/future focus to your reflection. So what will this change (now acknowledged) enable you to do (differently) in the future? This allows you to consider future possibilities from the secure basis of acknowledged development.

## Self-development through reflective writing

I have always found writing a fascinating process, as it allows me to gain a much more useful perspective on my thinking when I can see it written out on a page. This is a powerful advantage for reflective work. When ideas and thoughts are buzzing around in your head they bump into each other and can easily be hijacked or crushed by the continuous activity of thought. When you write about them you have to focus on specific concerns and give them your attention; also, when those thoughts or issues are down on paper they take on a more solid reality which has a certain separation from your thought process. You can then literally change your mind as you review what you have written. If you write in a slightly self-conscious way about something you have achieved, when you read it through you can simply acknowledge that you have done a good job: this can loop back to build your self-efficacy and expectation around further potential. Without capturing this as text, this possibility for self-development could be lost, as your old view of self continues, failing to acknowledge the professional progress you have made.

If you keep your reflective writing in an A4 notebook and watch it accumulate over a period of time (in my case a series of books covering about ten years) it becomes a useful resource, a way of tracking progress, providing insights on developments and on unhelpful habits that are still being worked on.

Dipping into my own archive I found the following back in February 1998. I had been through a very rough day at work and in my personal life. I had then travelled down to London because I was delivering training the next day. In the early evening I set and answered a brief series of questions:

Was I 'suffering'? – Yes, I was feeling hurt and neglected.
Was it useful? – Yes, it opened further areas for consideration.
Did I end up damaged? – No, I kept things going.
Did I 'die' of it? – No, it was not that important.

Two hours later I added the simple feedback statement:

'We survived!'

The reflective process worked by overstating my sense of the situation; it allowed my natural humour and playful irony to kick in and clear things.

Reflective writing did not come easily to me – my degree was in English Literature, I have always been fascinated with language and I had become expert at hiding behind words, so I could spin elegant text which flashed and impressed but actually had no reflective value. I failed to engage honestly with the topic to hand and instead built an elegant mask with the effort going into the creation of an accomplished piece of writing rather than honestly exploring my condition.

It may take time to find your voice or range of voices in reflective writing, but that simply requires patience and practice. Approached with a healthy curiosity about the variety of views you have about your own activity, reflective writing can become an exciting journey in self-exploration. Something that Alan Watts expresses far better than I can:

> The point, therefore of these arts, is doing them rather than the accomplishments. But more than this the real joy of them lies in what turns up unintentionally in the course of practice, just as the joy of travel is not nearly so much in getting where one wants to go as in the unsought surprises which occur on the journey.
>
> (Watts, 1957)

Your initial focus for reflective writing may be the narrow confines of a requirement to achieve professional acknowledgement by a professional body such as CILIP. However, human beings are notoriously dynamic in the way they work with their intelligence, and this process could happily spill over to allow you to glean powerful insights and learning which you will generalize to enhance your wider life.

All you need to do is start writing, and the process can begin.

# 4

## Curriculum vitae

### What is a CV?

A curriculum vitae (CV) may be defined as the story of your life but it is also an important statement about how you view yourself and a place for the projection of that view to others. Most of us will need to compile a CV at some stage in our career. Usually this will be to apply for a new job or for a promotion. There are many books and websites giving advice on the preparation of a CV for these purposes, including very useful guidance from CILIP at www.cilip.org.uk/jobs-careers/careers-gateway/life-at-work/interview/pages/cv.aspx. Much of this advice is useful if you are compiling a CV for the first time. The general rule is that you will need to compile a CV as soon as you leave education. You can store copies of your CV electronically; you might also find it useful to keep paper copies. Regularly review your CV to ensure that it is up to date and be prepared to re-present it to match the particular purposes/audiences that arise. Keeping your CV up to date is especially important as it is so much easier to record important events or changes in your career as they happen and not try to recall them from memory months or years later! Even if you are asked to complete an application form and not send a CV, your CV, if up to date, should provide most of the information you will need for filling out the form.

## The CV in your portfolio

Compiling your full CV is probably the best place to start when you are preparing your application for any CILIP qualification. It gives you an opportunity to record and review your knowledge and skills and to identify the key learning moments in your career to date. The CV in your portfolio is slightly different from one you would normally use for a job or promotion. You are not restricted in length and you can annotate the entries. However, a word of caution: assessors will not be happy with extra long CVs; generally two to four A4 pages would be a good rule, the final length obviously dependent on the range of your experience.

## Compiling your CV
### General

The style and layout of your CV is a personal choice but there are certain guidelines it is sensible to follow. Be concise, be confident (but honest), use only relevant information, and always give information in reverse chronological order, that is, the most recent first, whether you are talking about your experience, education or activities. The order of information in your CV will be your decision but there should be sections covering personal information (such as address details); knowledge and skills; work experience; education and training; professional activities; and, where appropriate, research undertaken and publications. Perhaps the most important thing to remember in compiling a CV for your portfolio is to make it easy for the assessor to know who you are and what you have done. Organize the information in a logical format and present the information clearly and concisely.

In your portfolio application you are required to submit a personal statement and this has a strict word limit; if you are concentrating on the last two to three years there may be key developmental activities from earlier in your life that you want to reflect on. You may annotate your CV to show these key learning outcomes or substantial achievements, for example taking part in a project or job outside of information and library work which developed your skills. Be brief, but show how this contributed to your professional development. Don't just describe what you did; think about the impact on you, your colleagues and the service.

All CVs should be word-processed and you should use a plain font no smaller than 12 point in size. Avoid any temptation to use lots of different fonts; one font and a judicious use of bold or italic is best.

## Introduction and personal profile

There should be a personal or introductory section which includes your name, address and contact details. There is some disagreement about also including with it a personal profile. This is a short paragraph – two or three sentences – highlighting your special qualities and skills. Most of us find it a section quite difficult to write and some employers/educators have expressed wariness about its use. However, it can be like that first 30 seconds in an interview and create a good first impression in the mind of the other person.

To prepare a personal profile, jot down three or four key things about yourself, for example:

I'm good with people.
I have excellent IT skills.
I have a lot of experience in finding information for users.

Then ask someone else to tell you, in no more than three sentences, what they admire about you or your work. Using these together, write a paragraph about yourself. Think about yourself as a product that you are marketing, or imagine you are travelling in a lift with the director of your company and that you have 45 seconds to tell her about yourself.

As is usually advised for introductions, this is probably best written after you have compiled the rest of your CV, even if it will actually appear very early on. Don't make any claims in this profile for which there is little supporting evidence in the body of the CV; for example, don't talk about being dynamic if nothing in your CV shows you as being dynamic. Also, if you do decide to use a personal profile – as with the rest of your CV – it will require regular updating!

## Key skills/qualities

For many job applications it is very useful to have a separate section which identifies your key skills and qualities. It can act as an extension of the personal profile, if you have included one, and be a very useful guide to the package which makes up the rest of your CV. It is also an area where you can cross-reference to your personal statement, your development plan and other evidence.

Some people prefer not to have a separate area on their CV for details of their skills and qualities but rather to integrate statements on key skills with the appropriate section on education or work experience. The choice is yours; however, by including it as a separate section, near the beginning of your CV, you are showing an ability to reflect on yourself and your abilities.

It is best to start the key skills section by listing your skills and qualities in draft; think about your technical or professional skills, inter-personal skills, your ability to work or lead a team; teaching skills; and any management skills, including finance. For help with articulating your knowledge and skills, look at the CILIP Body of Professional Knowledge (www.cilip.org.uk/jobs-careers/qualifications/accreditation/bpk/pages/default.aspx), and also look at the required skills as outlined in your job description.

When you have compiled this first draft try to quantify it as much as possible. Don't just use bland statements, mentioning, for example, that you have good IT skills – what exactly does that mean? If you say you are an experienced team leader, give examples. Whatever you identify here, remember to give evidence of it elsewhere in your CV.

## Work experience

This section is also sometimes referred to as employment history. Start with the most recent post and summarize the key responsibilities of each role you have held. Always take care to show the level, scope and scale. If you have decided to include a section on key skills/qualities, as mentioned above, do not repeat the information you have provided there in this section. Concentrate on your experience and any particular achievements (for example, running a successful event or receiving an award).

If appropriate, you can also include voluntary work and any relevant part-time work here. Try to select aspects of that work which have developed you as an information professional, for example, dealing with customers, designing a website or financial responsibilities.

## Education, qualifications and training

In this section give the details concisely and, as for the section above, in reverse chronological order. Keep annotation to a minimum in this section.

You may decide to separate the information into two sections, giving educational qualifications first and then any training you have undertaken. The decision is yours and will depend on the amount of information you wish to include. If you have recently completed a degree, at undergraduate or Master's level, and have written a dissertation as part of that course, you should include some information about it if the topic was relevant to library and information work. If you are studying for a higher degree you should also include details of the topic of your thesis.

Whether presented as a separate section or not, you should list all training undertaken, including in-house training and courses attended. Remember to give dates. If you are an experienced information professional, applying for Revalidation or Fellowship, and find that this list is very long, you may consider summarizing the information in this section and including a full list as part of the evidence you submit. Do not provide commentary in this part of your CV – you should demonstrate the outcomes of this training and any other professional development elsewhere in your portfolio.

## Professional activities

The emphasis in this section is on activity; it is an opportunity for you to outline the contribution you make to the profession. Membership of appropriate professional associations is expected; this must include CILIP, of course, but for many information professionals it is also important that we belong to other associations and institutions. Active participation should be detailed in this section. This can include attending meetings and conferences, locally or nationally, giving presentations, being on a committee, editing a website, being a mentor and so on. If you have a great deal of information to include in this section, it may be a good idea to subdivide it rather than just give a list by date; for example, you could split it into the sections CILIP branch or special interest group responsibilities, conferences, presentations and so forth.

## Publications

Give full bibliographic details of anything you have had published, including articles in newsletters or house journals. You can include conference papers or research projects in this section or, if preferred, list them in separate sections. If you are a less-experienced information professional it would be a good idea to include a copy of any article in your evidence; for those Members applying for Revalidation or Fellowship a detailed list is required here, with a sample of recent papers in the evidence.

## Other information

If you think that you have other relevant information to include in your CV which has not been covered in the sections listed above, you can consider having an additional section entitled 'Other information'. Often when applying for jobs it is usual to list other interests and activities, as this gives a rounded view. The information you include here should be relevant to your portfolio, however, and not be just a list of hobbies and interests. Participatory activities only should be included, and, if possible, you should reflect on the impact that the activities have made on you.

## Hints and tips

- ☛ Think about your skills and knowledge and make sure to bring these out in your CV.
- ☛ Store your CV electronically and keep it up to date.
- ☛ Divide your CV into meaningful sections.
- ☛ Always give information in reverse chronological order – latest first.
- ☛ Use a concise and clear style.
- ☛ Where appropriate, annotate your CV to show important learning or experience – but keep it short.
- ☛ Use your CV as a 'selling point' for your portfolio – the assessors do not know you so your CV should tell them a lot about you and your career.

## Conclusion

As with all elements in the portfolio, production of a CV enables you to identify key moments in your career and professional development and will make easier the task of matching your application to the criteria of assessment. Taking time with the structure and style will be repaid, as a well presented and carefully thought-through CV will act as a clear guide to the sort of information professional you are and create a good impression in the mind of others.

## CASE STUDY 4.1
### Karen Newton: My CV for Certification

For the first 27 years of my career I managed to get along fine without a CV; it never bothered me, I never bothered it, and we got along fine in ignorance of one other. Then one day CILIP launched the Certification of Affiliated Members and one of the main components within the portfolio for assessment was a CV – help!

OK, I thought, I can do this, after all, it's only a CV, it's nothing to be scared of, all I have to do is write down my career history in order of the most recent first, should be a doddle. The CV went something like this:

**1978–2005 •Library Assistant, Sunderland Public Libraries**

That was it – one employer for 27 years; the rest of the CV was simply blank, obviously not a good showcase of my skills and experiences!

## Developing my CV

Back to the drawing board, or, in my case, the husband. A few months previously his employer had relocated so far away that the commute was now six hours a day, so, after not too much thought, he opted for redundancy and, like myself, realized the need for a CV. 'Job Linkage' was based next door to the library I was working in, so he arranged a meeting and together they drafted a professional CV for him. So, not being one to reinvent the wheel – I pinched it! It was no use as it stood, of course, but I could 'borrow' the layout, the formatting and the overall look of it and adapt it for my own situation.

For what to include and how to have more than just the one line, I accessed the Infomatch website for how to complete a CV. They have lots of handy tips, including:

- Put the most relevant information first.
- Only put your education above work experience if you are a recent graduate, or if your qualification really is the most relevant aspect of your CV.
- Always list work experience and education in reverse chronological order, that is, starting with the most recent activity.

## Writing it all down

So, time to start getting it all down on paper. I wrote down all the positions I have held within Sunderland Libraries, encompassing the last 27 years, along with a brief outline of duties, concentrating on those which highlighted the aspects I wanted to relate to within the portfolio as a whole.

I started with the most recent, which at the time was:

## 2004–2006 •Assistant Manager, Hetton Library

- Organize and administer the running of a large branch library and oversee the running of two part-time branches.
- Lead a team of eight assistants.
- Liaise with other departments within the building under the banner of 'People First'.
- Supervise all financial and budget transactions.
- Manage a programme of further education courses, both accredited and vocational.
- Allocation of staff timetabling and annual leave.
- Monitor and report on targets.

And ended with my first post at 16 years old, which was:

## 1978–1983 •Library Assistant

- Issue and return of stock.
- Shelving and repair of stock.
- Day-to-day issue-desk duties.

I kept the early years of my career relatively basic. However, for the later parts of my career there was much more to include and make reference to within my portfolio.

My education was along similar lines; one village school until I was 11, and then on to grammar school for O-levels – but once I had left school and started work, there was much more to add. In fact on my CV there is only one line on education, which says:

## 1973–1978 •Houghton Grammar School, County Durham

- Seven O-levels

And that's the total of my pre-employment educational history, as it is just that – ancient history.

*Training*

More recent and, to my mind, much more relevant, is the training and education I have undergone since I left school, from health and safety courses to communications workshops undertaken in-house, to a City and Guilds Library and Information Assistants Certificate taken by day release at the College of Arts and Technology, Newcastle. This could all be backed up by the evidence of certificates in my portfolio, and these certificates came in very handy when I had to work out exactly when it was that I had attended the course.

*Professional activities*

When it came to writing down my professional activities and the publications that I had contributed to, there were more than I initially thought. I obviously enjoy working in a library, which came as a bit of a surprise! These were added to my CV as well – once again in reverse chronological order, with the most recent first. But don't think that by 'professional activities' I mean just working with CILIP; make sure that any project work you have helped with is included, such as refurbishments or reorganizations, major stock edits, promotional work, for example, the Summer Reading Challenge and so on. You should also list any relevant experience outside of work – for example, committee or unpaid work, treasurer for the parent–teacher association or volunteering as a Brownie pack leader. And also include staff newsletters and web pages.

## Conclusion

My CV was finally completed. It was too long for a normal CV, but was not to be used for a job application; it was to be used to demonstrate my abilities and knowledge, and would, hopefully, go towards a successful ACLIP portfolio. One of the main things to remember when compiling a CV in this case is that there is no size or word restriction. Usually a CV has a maximum of two pages; in this instance it can be longer to include a lot of additional information that may not fit into the size-restricted personal statement and development plan. You can cross-reference from your CV to the portfolio contents, but I found that it did not work well for me; it looked more messy than informative.

So how have we got on together since then? Quite well thank you. We go out together to various events, and once I even sent it off all by itself for an actual job application. Oh and I've taken Infomatch's advice and keep it up to date with regular rewrites, so it always looks fresh and current – just like its owner on a good day.

## CASE STUDY 4.2
### Margaret Watson: My CV for Fellowship

When I finally committed myself to applying for Fellowship of CILIP in 2003 I did wonder where I should start. I did have lots of 'stuff' – hard copies of documents and electronic files – and a vague idea of the themes I wanted to concentrate on. I had decided to make my application based on the contribution I believe I had made to Library and Information Studies education, in particular in ensuring the integration of theory and practice, and on the contribution I had made to the profession. Being a very practical person I decided to start on the obvious, and what I thought might be the 'easiest' part of the portfolio – revising my CV.

Because of the work involved in the revision of my CV and reflecting on my career to date, I found this a very useful 'kick start' to the whole business of making my application. I also quite enjoyed looking back at some of my earlier CVs and job applications. There were some things I had forgotten all about! I also became aware of a pattern which I perhaps would not have otherwise discovered: my career was not planned in a formal way, but clearly information literacy and dealing with users provided the basis of much of my work. This interest in helping users find the information they required eventually developed into teaching library and information studies. Reflecting on the way my career had developed, the choices I had made and the decision to be an active member of my professional association was useful in preparing the whole application.

Back to the work on the CV! The university where I taught required all staff to keep an up-to-date CV in electronic form and in a very specific format. However, apart from qualifications, the university CV was only to cover the last five years. So when I looked at my current CV it was only a starting point. I had been a Chartered Librarian since 1967, so a great deal had happened in those intervening years. Fortunately I had kept e-copies of CVs I had used to apply for promotion within the university and I also had paper copies of earlier CVs from when I had applied for other jobs. So my first task was to assemble a master CV. This is my first piece of advice – don't do what I did – do as I say! Keep your CV up to date at all times and have a master CV which you can then use or adapt to meet the circumstances. I needed a much fuller CV than the one I was using and it was quite a task to get it organized properly.

## Annotating the CV

One of the major problems of submitting my Fellowship so late in my career was that there was such a lot of information I could include. It was perfectly obvious that the 500-word limit on the personal statement meant that I had to focus very clearly and not include information which was peripheral to the submission. I discussed the problem of trying to put a gallon into a pint pot with a friend, who just replied, 'Annotate the CV.' It was one of those light-bulb moments! This meant that I could highlight important elements in my career or personal development in the CV and not need to include them in the other parts of the portfolio. The CV could then really be the story of my career, which would be part of the evidence I used to address the assessment criteria.

Two examples of this use of annotating my CV came from earlier posts:

**1979–1987 •Assistant Librarian, Humanities, Sunderland Polytechnic**
I had responsibility for collection development, online information retrieval and user education in eight subject disciplines and achieved a high level of success in liaising with academic staff.

**1968–1972 •Assistant Librarian and Information Officer, University of Newcastle upon Tyne**
I became the first Information Officer and was responsible for introducing the first user education programme across the university.

These statements provided a link between my earlier work and the focus in my personal statement on education and training of library and information professionals.

I also listed a wide variety of professional activity over the last 20 years and added the following notation:

> Professional activity over the last 16 years has informed my teaching and research and has enabled me to bring together practitioners and educators in our discipline.

This statement picked up points I was making in my personal statement and for which I had other supporting evidence.

## Organizing the CV

I decided to organize my CV into seven sections:

- Personal information – name and status.
- Qualifications.
- Employment – this was the largest section and needed to be very clearly set out. My last post had two distinct elements: one, the work I did in the subject department as principal lecturer, and the other, the work I did within the wider university. I briefly annotated the entries where appropriate.
- Professional activities – I included a couple of annotations here.
- Research and consultancy.
- Courses and conferences – I divided this section into two: first, course/conferences I had organized or spoken at and, second, those I had attended.
- Publications.

It is important to remember that the assessors who look at your application only see what you have presented to them. They do not know you so it is crucial that they can look at your CV and get a real feeling for you as an information professional. The CV is a very valuable part of your supporting evidence. As with everything in my application I asked my husband to read my CV. He is not a librarian so it was very useful to get an objective opinion.

## Keeping the CV up to date

So what have I done with my CV since getting my Fellowship? As I am now retired, why should I bother? As I am still involved with training mentors and assessors I need to make sure that I keep my knowledge and skills up to date so that I have credibility in the profession. Through CILIP I have also become involved in new areas of work such as diversity and ethics, so am still learning. So I have compiled a 'master' CV without the annotations and try to keep that up to date. I have also set up a folder on my PC in which I can store any relevant documents, such as evaluations and course information. I have found the revalidation audit sheet really useful to help me to reflect on professional activities, but have to admit that I don't use it as much as I should; I still keep a big box to store hard copy 'evidence'. So the verdict is 'Can still do better'!

# 5

## Professional development plans

I have included in this chapter discussion of the personal development plan (PDP) for Certification candidates, the personal professional development plan (PPDP) for Chartership candidates and the CPD log for Revalidation candidates. The common element for all these documents is planning your development.

### What is a PDP?

Any personal professional development plan is essential to the role we all have in the information business. Because the work is continually changing and our roles change quite frequently it is important to be able to plan your continuing personal and professional development. You need to consider CPD as not something that just happens to you in an unstructured way, but rather as something in which you are proactive, determining your goals and how you are going to reach them. CPD should be planned in such a way that your knowledge and skills are enhanced and improved by a programme of varied developmental activities. By formally recording your CPD you can track your development and think about the next steps: 'Personal planning provides direction, sets out objectives, identifies potential areas of development. It should not confine the individual; it must be flexible in order to accommodate unexpected opportunities and newly discovered skills and abilities; and must be regularly reviewed' (Webb and Grimwood-Jones,

2003). All through your career you will need to identify your developmental needs for the work you do, for your future work, for your employer and for yourself. For your CILIP qualification you will need to identify any development needs to meet the assessment criteria.

## Skills and knowledge audit

Before you start any development plan you need to carry out an audit of your skills and knowledge. In other words, you need to know where you are starting from, where you want to go and how you will get there.

Sometimes the easiest place to start in your audit is to look closely at your job description. Check that you have the necessary skills and knowledge and record them. Consider any other duties you carry out in addition to the job specification; record the skills and knowledge that enable you to carry out those roles. Then think about other skills you have which are not, perhaps, part of your everyday work. Following all of this analysis, consider whether there are any gaps in your skills and knowledge that would enable you to do your job more effectively. It may just be updating your skills, or your job may recently have changed and you need to acquire a different skill set or more knowledge about a certain area of work.

Another way of starting is to carry out a SWOT (strengths, weaknesses, opportunities, threats) analysis; identify your strengths and weaknesses and any 'threats', which in CPD terms are the demands that you will be facing in the coming months. The 'opportunities' here will be the steps you can take to overcome those 'threats'. Consult one or two trusted colleagues and ask them to do an informal SWOT analysis on you. Ask them to tell you three things you do well and three things you can improve on. If you have performance review or appraisal schemes at work you will be asked to identify training and development needs. Use the record of these meetings to help you with planning your development activities. As well as the advice from CILIP mentors and events run by CILIP, there are useful tools on the web to help you plan your personal development, including TFPL's Knowledge and Information Skills Toolkit and Recording Skills Development for ILS Skills Portfolio.

## Setting goals

Once you know where you are starting from, you need to think about setting goals. Most writers on this topic suggest using SMART goals. The goals you set yourself (or in the case of an appraisal, are set for you, or in consultation with you) should be:

- **s**pecific
- **me**asurable
- **a**ttainable
- **r**elevant
- **t**imed.

In other words, do not set yourself unrealistic and vague goals which you probably can't achieve, will be difficult to measure and have no time limit on them. It is better to aim for five or six very clearly defined targets which are achievable, normally within a year, rather than a wide-sweeping CPD plan. After all, the plan is dynamic and not set in stone. Life happens, work changes, and you may need to plot a different course. I remember in one appraisal being asked to identify my development needs; having been through quite good appraisal training I tried to set realistic goals, knowing what the new academic year would bring. Within three months of drawing up my plan, I found myself in a totally different and unexpected situation where my development needs were thoroughly changed. But once you get into the habit of thinking logically about your CPD that sort of shift should not be too difficult.

## Development activity

Having set your goals, then of course you must consider how you are going to achieve them. Remember that reaching your goal does not necessarily mean going on a course! You should use a wide range of activities to help in your development; these can include shadowing, attending meetings, chairing meetings, assisting in training, coaching other colleagues, reading, writing reports, project work and professional activities.

Always record your developmental activity but also try to reflect on how well it has gone. What were the initial outcomes for you? What were the outcomes six months later? (See Chapter 3 for more ideas on reflective writing.)

If you get into good habits early on in your career none of this recording and reflecting will seem difficult. What is usually difficult is to start, especially if you are at a point quite late on in your career. I speak from experience! When I first started out, no one told me how useful it would be to record my professional development. Like many people, I began to do it only when the job demanded it. I had evaluated training and development but only in an informal way, and generally immediately after the event. I had evidence of successful career development, but not in any organized way. Fortunately the university where I worked introduced a very good appraisal scheme where you had to reflect on the last 12 months and identify your development needs. Recording and reflecting on your development will help you both in your career and when you apply for a CILIP qualification.

## Certification

Your PDP is about forward thinking. When you are submitting your portfolio you need to identify what you are going to do next. Your ACLIP application is about reflecting on your achievements to date and the PDP is looking ahead to maintaining and enhancing your skills and knowledge. You can also include activities which you are currently undertaking. For example, you may need to know more about reading development or helping customers to use the internet. One of the targets you might include would be moving on to Chartership after you have gained your ACLIP! If you do decide to go on to Chartership then your PDP should prove a very valuable tool. There are examples of PDPs from successful applications on the CILIP website and some thoughts on how to approach your PDP later in this chapter.

## Hints and tips

☞ Discuss your plan with your mentor or line manager.

☞ Write down what you are good at in your job.

☞ Identify what you can do to improve those skills and knowledge.

☞ Think about the next 12 months at work – are there any new developments in the service you will need to know about or any new areas of work you will have to undertake?

☞ Set yourself four or five realistic targets with a stated time for completion.

☞ Think about how you will know that the targets and your own learning outcomes have been met.

☞ Attend a Certification event.

☞ Join the ACLIP discussion list.

## Chartership

> The process of putting together a Personal Professional Development Plan is a valuable exercise in identifying training needs and appropriate learning and developmental activities and is a useful tool for ongoing career planning beyond Chartership.
>
> (Marshall, 2006)

The Chartership PPDP is not rocket science! It is intended to record where you are at the beginning of the registration process, where you need to get to, and the actions you intend to take in order to get there. It does not have to be complicated. Your PPDP should form the basis of the first meeting you have with your mentor. Together you can discuss the various activities you will need to undertake during the registration period. You e-mail your PPDP to CILIP but that first PPDP is not what you submit with your portfolio. The first version and the portfolio version will not be the same because your development plan will change over the period of preparing your application. Your PPDP is dynamic and reflects your personal growth over the whole period. You and your mentor will return several times to check on progress and make changes as appropriate to you and your work.

Before starting on your PPDP undertake the audit of knowledge and skills as described above. Read the Body of Professional Knowledge (BPK) and think about the areas you need to find out more about and the skills you need to enhance. Applying for Chartership is not about being able to do everything and knowing all that there is to know about information work – it is about showing your ability to develop from your first qualification and a commitment to improvement and enhancement.

If you are submitting an application for Chartership when you have already been working for some years you may need to change the format of your PPDP slightly. Your mentor will advise you on this. Briefly, you will need to concentrate on the period of registration, but you may wish also to submit a record of earlier CPD which has contributed to your growth as an information professional.

## Hints and tips

- ☞ Prepare a draft PPDP and discuss it with your mentor.
- ☞ Set SMART goals.
- ☞ Be prepared to adapt your plan as circumstances change.
- ☞ Attend a Chartership event.
- ☞ Join the Chartership discussion list.
- ☞ Read the Body of Professional Knowledge.
- ☞ Evaluate all training and development activities.
- ☞ Review your progress regularly with your mentor.
- ☞ Update your PPDP regularly.

## Revalidation

When you start on the process of Revalidation you will need to carry out a skills audit if you have not already done so for work. You will need to plan your CPD based on that audit. Revalidation is normally a three-year cycle. Each year you will need to complete an interim CPD log and then complete a final CPD log for your portfolio in year three. If you are an experienced information professional you can, in the first instance, apply for Revalidation immediately by submitting your portfolio, including the CPD log which can cover several years. The CPD log is a required element and it is a straightforward record of all CPD activity. If you have undertaken many CPD activities, I suggest you group them into themes, for example: management development, information literacy, web development and so on.

Importantly, I also suggest you use the CPD audit sheet as the tool to help you identify your learning outcomes and evaluate all your training and development activity. This completed audit provides a useful item of evidence for your portfolio.

It is important for Revalidation that you undertake a wide range of activities. The activities undertaken for Revalidation are not at all prescriptive and will depend on the role you have and the context in which you work. As with Certification and Chartership, you can begin with an audit of skills and knowledge. Set yourself SMART goals or realistic learning outcomes for the 12 months ahead and use the audit sheet to monitor and record any improvements or enhancements to your knowledge and skills. You should be able to incorporate your CILIP Revalidation into any performance review or appraisal scheme you have at work. But don't forget your CILIP Revalidation is also about personal growth, so you may choose to include CPD activities not directly related to your specific role. For example, many information professionals choose to study for a higher degree not directly related to their role but which may be relevant to include because of the research and other skills used.

## Hints and tips

- ☞ Use the audit sheet to help you evaluate your CPD activity.
- ☞ If you want to cite many examples of CPD activity organize those activities into themes.
- ☞ Update your CPD log regularly.
- ☞ Update and review your audit sheet regularly.

···················································································

CASE STUDY 5.1
**Sarah Cockroft, Roberta Crossley and Heather Karpicki: The PDP for Certification**

···················································································

Five librarians from Calderdale Libraries worked together on the new single category ACLIP applications. They all had a great deal of prior experience in libraries or related work.

## Personal development plan

Having worked for Calderdale Libraries for a considerable number of years we felt that we ought to do something to cement our knowledge and experience. Most of us had done the City and Guilds Library and Information course but had gone no further with professional qualifications. The ACLIP single category proved to be a great way of doing this and after attending a workshop promoting the new certification we all signed up to complete our ACLIP portfolio and with a lot of expert help from mentors were soon on our way to completion.

I think it is fair to say that we found working on the personal development plan difficult. It was good to refer to our annual appraisals and to identify any training and development that was needed. But we also found that checking through the Service Improvement Plan was a good way of looking at the type of things we could be involved with in the future. When we submitted our draft work to our line manager as well, then helpful suggestions were made about our development.

By carefully reflecting on what we had done and achieved it became clear that a pattern was emerging of our strengths which gave us a good idea of the type of things we could 'specialize' in. The first part of the personal development plan was a good confidence-builder, as you are required to list your key tasks and responsibilities and outline aspects of your role. Within these parameters, areas of training requirements were identified and proposed actions were set. The task really acted as a 'signpost' to gaps in our training but also made us aware that we have to push boundaries to move on in our careers.

Overall, the process of putting together our portfolio and gaining the ACLIP status has been a positive thing for all of us. We are all proud of attaining the qualification and it is great to have recognized all of the experience and knowledge that we have gained throughout our careers. For one reason or another there are people who do not go the way of formal qualifications but have all the necessary experience anyway to 'do the job'. It's great to be part of a larger professional organization and to be able to access all of the opportunities and help that this provides. The fact that the ACLIP single category is available shows that CILIP is an organization that is moving and changing with the times. For this we are all grateful for the opportunity given to us.

## CASE STUDY 5.2
### Lesley Randall: My PPDP for Chartership

In April 2005 I was pleased to discover a new qualification – ACLIP, which recognizes the contribution made in library and information work by para-professionals like me, so I joined CILIP and started the process towards ACLIP accreditation, which I was awarded in March 2007.

## The value of Certification

ACLIP is like a foundation course because it prepared the way for me to start evaluating what I was doing within the library service and to look 'outside the box' at the bigger picture. The Personal Development Plan template was important in this process of focusing on my training and development needs and formulating an action plan and timescale in order to achieve it all in. I also had to indicate how I would develop my participation within the profession. Being a Member of CILIP started the ball rolling as it increased my knowledge of training and opportunities within the profession and opened doors to other events and activities. CILIP Members' Day is valuable as there are always good workshops to attend and ample opportunity to find out the latest about what the organization has to offer and how you can get involved. Through networking at this event I was featured in an article in *Library and Information Gazette* 'The Sum of all Experiences' (January 2007). This was a 'tour de force' in describing my professional development – a good synopsis of my personal performance and diversity of working practices – demonstrating the inadequacy of the title 'Librarian'. The ACLIP PDP and subsequent portfolio work made this article possible as the whole process had increased my confidence and awareness of what I had to offer and my transferrable skills.

## The value of mentoring

Through the mentoring process I developed as a professional practioner, gaining knowledge and experience that I couldn't have acquired elsewhere. Having a mentor working in a different sector at the British Library was very important, allowing for the cross-fertilization of ideas, networking and a sharing of information. My mentor's network enabled me to expand my contacts and organize meetings and take responsibility for my own development. My mentor supported me through Chartership too, and our meetings were invaluable for focused discussions, where I began to lead, reflect and evaluate. This gave me the confidence and experience to reflect critically on my personal performance and be more engaged with evaluating service performance.

## The PPDP

The PPDP (Personal Professional Development Plan) for Chartership mapped my progress and developmental activities since ACLIP accreditation. The Assessment Panel for my ACLIP portfolio identified two points I particularly need to focus on: 1) achieving a better understanding of critical evaluation of working practices and service objectives, and 2) gaining practice in reflective writing. These became key objectives that fed the rest of the PPDP. My Professional Activities and Training Log for Chartership shows how I achieved the first by participation in extensive and wide ranging meetings, visits and events that provided me with a broader perspective of working practices and service objectives. I realized that things are changing at a rapid pace within the library and information profession and that I need to continually keep up to date in order to be able to evaluate critically and put forward my own opinions. To achieve the second objective, I started to keep a diary at work and made time to reflect on anything I felt might be useful for the portfolio. Meetings with my mentor were invaluable in evaluating the activities we discussed. Similarly, recording information in the mentoring log was another opportunity to focus on key developments and what to do next. Write-ups immediately after an activity have been imperative to reflective practice. Because of these activities I have been more empowered at 'performance related pay' meetings with my manager, as well as becoming more confident about what I have achieved, what I have to offer and how I shall accomplish my training needs.

## Professional practice

The Personal Professional Development Plan for Chartership helped me to chart my progress and identify key areas to be addressed. Increased awareness of the information sector through visits and in-house training focused my perspective and the urge to develop my career. I also became more proactive with CILIP activities and groups and began to visit other organizations and different sectors/boroughs. Regular reading of professional literature ensured awareness of current issues and how I could get involved.

Pathway 2 was my chosen route to Chartership and should cover two years (full-time) equivalent professional practice. The handbook states that 'normally this will be in a designated professional post. However, it is the professional content of the job that matters and how it will help you to meet the criteria for assessment, rather than simply the job title.' This is an important point – although I already had a lot of experience, I hadn't actually identified the 'professional content' of what I was doing. The PPDP helps you to address this and continuing professional development helps you to identify your qualities and skills in a completely different way.

In my role as Senior Library Assistant I don't have direct involvement in strategy and policy making; however my contribution to the service has been positive at all levels and is reflected in my yearly performance appraisals. Commitment to active professional development furthers my understanding and knowledge, enabling me to contribute more effectively to a quality library service for all.

## Conclusion

In September 2009, an e-mail confirmed that the portfolio I submitted for Chartership had been successful. It has been a long journey, but well worth the trip! It has been very important for me to be able to do things at my own pace, and my personal progression has been energizing and empowering in ways that I couldn't have envisaged at the outset. A turning point has been in becoming a committee member of CILIP in London, and I will take on an unexpected role of editing their newsletter in the New Year. There is also the opportunity to get involved in website content. I am becoming more of a 'professional activist' to gain skills and experience in areas that I cannot achieve in the current job and also to give something back to the profession and CILIP organization. I now need to revise my PPDP to move on to the next level!

# 6

## Personal statements

### What is a personal statement?

In many ways the personal statement is the most important element in your portfolio. I think of it rather like an executive summary in a report. If the report is long you should be able to get a very good idea of its contents from the summary. The executive summary almost stands as a document by itself. People should be able to read your personal statement and understand immediately what you are presenting about yourself and your career. The personal statement is the one piece of reflective writing that *must* be in your portfolio, although hopefully there will be other examples in the supporting evidence too. Your personal statement should show evidence of analysis, evaluation and review of your knowledge and experience. You will need to have all the other evidence in place so that you can write an informative and reflective statement.

### Initial drafting

You will probably need at least two or three drafts before you are satisfied with your personal statement. The first draft I prepared for my Fellowship application was no good at all; it was really just a narrative version of my CV. However, writing it like that got it out of my system and helped me to concentrate on what I really wanted to say. Ultimately, I found it very useful to build my statement around the assessment criteria.

You will find it useful to discuss the early drafts of your personal statement with your mentor or a 'buddy', as they may have a more objective view. As a mentor I have found that most people are reluctant to 'boast' of their success and accomplishments.

However it comes into fruition, remember that the assessor will not know you and may not be familiar with your organization, so you have to make the personal statement purposeful and focused. But also beware – do not make any statements that are not substantiated by what is contained in the rest of the portfolio. The easiest way to do this is to cross-reference the points you are making to the evidence, whether that is in the CV, the supporting letter(s) or the other evidence you have brought together.

## Certification

You need to download a copy of the personal statement template from: www.cilip.org.uk/jobs-careers/qualifications/cilip-qualifications/certification/pages/certificationforms.aspx.

Do read the guidance notes carefully before you start to fill in the form. The template lists the criteria and then prompts you to provide the necessary information. Each section must be completed, although you may have different amounts of information for each criterion. You will also need to provide a short summary of your overall development. As well as the guidance notes and prompts on the template there are further guidance notes available on the website which give you more information on each section. In the left-hand column of the template you can list your developmental activities; it is a good idea to include cross-references to the evidence in your portfolio for each activity in that left-hand column too. In the right-hand column you need to reflect on the activity or event.

For the first criterion you are asked to evaluate both your own personal performance and the performance of your service. When you are thinking about evaluating your own performance think about your personal effectiveness in delivering the service. Over the last year, what do you feel has gone well and what might have been improved? Can you see any difference in your work now as opposed to how it was 12 months ago?

You should use any appraisal notes from your line manager to help you. Don't forget you will need evidence to support what you are saying. This evidence is also important when evaluating service performance so any survey results, feedback from users, letters and e-mails can be useful. The personal statement is your document so should reflect what you honestly feel; it should not just be a bland statement.

The second criterion addresses specifically your acquisition of new or updated skills. It can include formal and informal training, project work and learning on the job – in fact any activity from which you have learned. You then need to reflect on the outcomes of that training or development activity.

For the third criterion you need to think about the wider community; for example how does your information unit fit into the mission of the organization, or how does your school library support the school policy, or how does your branch library contribute to the wider community? You should be able to think of examples of how the library benefits its users and look for evidence to support your claims, for example, events that are held in the library to encourage more reading or programmes of activities for specific age groups.

It is a good idea to spend some time with your mentor discussing the personal statement and to work on at least two or three drafts. You will also get more help from attending a Certification event. Talking to someone else about your statement can help you to articulate what is most important and help to clarify your ideas. This is particularly important when compiling the summary. Remember that the draft can be as long as you want but the final version of your personal statement can only be a maximum of four A4 pages, including the summary! So be concise and avoid descriptive writing. See Figure 6.1.

## Chartership

You are required to produce a personal evaluative statement for your Chartership portfolio. This statement has a maximum of 1000 words. In the handbook it is very clearly linked to the assessment criteria and to a focus on the outcomes of your developmental activities. The personal

**Criterion 1: (Candidates must demonstrate) an ability to evaluate personal performance and service performance**

| | Reflections and evaluation |
|---|---|
| a) **Personal performance** *(give examples of your performance)* | *What went well? How successful were you in achieving your own objectives? What might have gone better?* |
| | |
| | |
| | *Add or delete rows as necessary.* |
| b) **Service performance** *(give examples for your service)* | *How well is your information/library service performing? Are the aims/objectives/targets met? How can improvements be made?* |
| | |
| | |
| | |
| | *Add or delete rows as necessary* |

**Criterion 2: (Candidates must demonstrate) an understanding of the ways in which their personal, technical and professional skills have developed through training and developmental activities and/or through practice**

| **Activity** *(training and development and/or work experience)* | **Reflections** – *What did you learn from the activity? How did you use what you learned? How did your work benefit? How did you benefit? Was your learning need met or did/do you need more support or training?* |
|---|---|
| | |
| | |
| | *Add or delete rows as necessary.* |

**Criterion 3: (Candidates must demonstrate) an appreciation of the role of library and information services in the wider community** *('wider community' may be interpreted as the information/library service, the employing organization, or other community as appropriate)*

| **Role and contribution** *(give examples for your service)* | **Involvement, evaluation and success** – *How does your service 'fit' into the wider context? What are the benefits? ... to your service?... to other providers?... to users? Outline and evaluate any partnership working or other collaborative projects.* |
|---|---|
| | |
| | |
| | *Add or delete rows as necessary.* |

**UMMARY (maximum 250 words)**
lease provide an overall assessment of your development and how it has benefited you and/or the service in which you work:

**Figure 6.1** Certification template

statement links all of the elements of your portfolio together. As mentioned at the beginning of this chapter, it is really the executive summary of your portfolio. It summarizes and reflects on your professional development since qualification or Certification.

By the time you write your evaluative statement you will have amassed a great deal of evidence. You will have gained more work experience, perhaps attended conferences, courses or in-house training; you may have been involved in a project, visited other information services, participated in professional activities, and in many other developmental activities. You need to show how any evidence you are submitting meets the assessment criteria. A relatively easy way to map out your evidence and to ensure that you meet the criteria is to use a matrix as shown in Figure 6.2.

| Activity | Criterion 1 | Criterion 2 | Criterion 3 | Criterion 4 | Evidence |
|----------|-------------|-------------|-------------|-------------|----------|
| | Ability to reflect critically on personal performance and to evaluate service performance. | Active commitment to CPD. | Ability to analyse personal and professional development with reference to experiential and developmental activities. | Breadth of professional knowledge and understanding of the wider professional context. | |
| For example: Attending Umbrella Conference. | PARTLY YES – had to evaluate outcomes for myself. | YES – needed to update on Web 2.0. Part of PPDP. | YES – was able to network and have contacts for future Web 2.0 development. | YES – new contacts in other sectors. | Report to home organization. Article for branch newsletter. |

**Figure 6.2** Evidence matrix

The criteria form one axis and the developmental activities the other. You can then cross-reference all your evidence and all your developmental activities to the criteria. Remember that not all activities will meet all of the criteria – that's fine, so long as you have a good balance overall. When you look at the completed matrix you should be able to see the pattern of your evaluative statement emerge. You can then divide your evaluative statement into sections covering an introduction and the four criteria, and can then show how your supporting evidence demonstrates that you meet all of the criteria. Hopefully, by doing it this way you can avoid simply describing what you have done.

This is only a suggestion – don't forget that the portfolio belongs to you and is a personal and unique account of your professional development. You can get lots of advice from your mentor and from your local Candidate Support Officer and you should find the time to attend at least one Chartership event.

## Fellowship

Talking to colleagues who have applied for their Fellowship, everyone seems to agree that the 500-word personal statement proved one of the most difficult things they ever had to write. As mentioned earlier, many of us struggle to write about our own achievements. Sometimes it really helps to discuss it with someone else. When I realized how poor my first attempt at the personal statement was, I discussed it with my husband and with a professional colleague. They challenged me to rethink how I was approaching it. Other colleagues have got together in small groups and become a mutual support network. You should find that in explaining something to another person it forces you to clarify your ideas.

Each personal statement is unique and the claims that each of us make are very different. However, I feel that the common factor is the necessity to reflect and focus on the key issues. Look at the assessment criteria, decide on the reasons why you are applying, choose two to five of these reasons and build your statement around them. I have found it very interesting to work with colleagues who are thinking about applying for Fellowship and to get them to focus on their achievements. You may also find using a matrix, as described in the Chartership section, helpful to map the evidence against the criteria so that you can use the personal statement as a signpost to the rest of your portfolio.

## Revalidation

As it says in the Revalidation handbook, 'your personal statement will be a personal evaluation and reflection on the CPD that you have under-

taken since gaining Chartership or your previous Revalidation'. So if
you have kept a CPD audit sheet, as shown in Figure 6.3 (www.cilip.org.uk/
jobs-careers/qualifications/cilip-qualifications/revalidation/pages/
revalidationform.aspx), you should already have reflected on each development activity undertaken during the qualifying period.

| Date | Activity | What you learned from the activity | How you applied it in the workplace |
|------|----------|-----------------------------------|-------------------------------------|
|      |          |                                   |                                     |
|      |          |                                   |                                     |

**Figure 6.3** CPD audit sheet

Before you prepare your personal statement you can organize your activities into larger groupings and draw out the main learning outcomes.

## Hints and tips

☛ Decide on the key points you want to make in your personal
statement.

☛ Keep it clear and concise.

☛ Do not just describe what you have done – evaluate and review
your development. Use the 'so what?' principle.

☛ Cross-reference to other elements in your portfolio.

☛ Look at examples of statements on the CILIP website.

☛ Discuss drafts with your mentor or a 'buddy'.

☛ Go to an event run specifically for the award to which you are
submitting your portfolio.

☛ Remind yourself of the assessment criteria.

CASE STUDY 6.1
**Calderdale Libraries: Sarah Cockcroft, Roberta Crossley and
Heather Karpicki: The personal statement for Certification**

Five librarians from Calderdale Libraries worked together on the new single category ACLIP applications. They all had a great deal of prior experience in libraries or related work.

## Writing the personal statement

Having worked for Calderdale Libraries for a considerable number of years we felt that we ought to do something to cement our knowledge and experience. Most of us had done the City and Guilds Library and Information course but had gone no further with gaining professional qualifications. The ACLIP single category seemed to be a great way of changing this situation and after attending a workshop promoting the new Certification, we all signed up to complete our ACLIP portfolio and, with a lot of expert help from mentors, were soon on our way to completion.

It was really important to focus on what we had achieved, what we can achieve and what we hope to achieve. We had to learn to reflect on what we had learnt from our various working experiences. It wasn't easy at first to do this as we were initially far too descriptive, something which is perhaps natural when you want to make clear how tasks were achieved to someone who doesn't know what you have done. It is not sufficient, however, to say 'I achieved this and this is how I did it'; we had to think about how it changed us and made us more confident in accepting new challenges. We also had to show how we approached things differently when dealing with similar situations, thus showing how we had grown and matured. Throughout this we gained an overview of how we have each developed and how our past experiences have paved the way for the roles we now fulfil.

## Matching the assessment criteria

A valuable time was when we all met together with our mentors to share the things we had done as this prompted us to remember additional things we had forgotten about. The difficulty was matching the evidence with the assessment criteria, as it appeared that some of the criteria could overlap, but that was fine. We found that one example could fit in with service development as well as personal development. The important thing was to choose examples of work experience and then be concise in stating what we had learnt and how we grew in confidence.

We needed evidence to go with our statements so it was important to choose carefully the examples we were giving. In many ways, once you have started the process of reflection the difficulty of completing the form is not what to include, but rather what to leave out, and how to edit down all the information you have. It makes you realize just how varied your job is and how wide your skill set has developed as a result.

The templates of the personal statement should give you the direction you need, but it is worthwhile getting into the habit of writing evaluations of events, workshops or training as well as any particular problems you have dealt with. Print off any correspondence that might be useful to support what you are stating has happened, such as what a colleague may have sent you in support of some work project you have done, particularly anything praising and acknowledging your input.

## The mentors

The mentors gave valuable advice and offered constructive criticism of where we needed to change things. The key things we learnt we had to remember are:

- Keep it brief and be concise and not too descriptive – remember the statement is about you and how you reacted and what you learnt.
- Get into a reflective mentality, always questioning, 'What did I learn?', 'How have I grown?', 'What do I do different now?'
- Cross-reference at every opportunity to make sure that mention is made of all the evidence you have used.
- Save anything that might be useful – e-mails, newspaper cuttings, programmes of events you have organized, thank-you notes, photographs, examples of anything you have done to help improve the service, be that creating a simple form or putting workshop material together.
- Remember to de-personalize any examples you put in your portfolio.
- Don't overload your portfolio with evidence but make the evidence you

have work for you. You can use a good piece of evidence to cover a couple of statements.

- Stick to the assessment criteria.
- Be professional when putting your portfolio together – no scruffy handwritten labels.
- Think carefully about the layout of your portfolio and try to put it together always thinking that someone will be reading it who doesn't know who you are or the full nature of your job.
- Set out the evidence references against your statements clearly.
- Use your mentor.

## Moving on

The personal statement template also helps to identify the areas of development and training you still require in order to move into new work experiences. A valuable lesson learnt was that we gained an overview of our strengths and likely future development. We also understood more about seeing the 'bigger picture', not only of how our work fits in with the service as a whole but also in terms of seeing a more rounded view of ourselves as people.

## CASE STUDY 6.2
**Paul Tovell: Writing the evaluative statement for my Chartership portfolio**

I never wanted my Chartership assessors to read my diary. But that notebook carefully hidden many years ago was the last time I had dabbled in reflective writing. If only I had kept it up, I found myself thinking after my Chartership workshop, the evaluative statement of my portfolio would be easy. Instead, the prospect of 'reflecting' was now a daunting one. Not only did I feel alarmed at the thought of submitting something so personal, but also there were so many ways it could go wrong. Reflective writing can be repetitive and irrelevant, and the word limit left no room for waffle. This was my big chance to demonstrate professional competence – it was definitely not the place for vague sentiments like 'I enjoyed my day out because it was nice.'

Apprehensively, I contacted my mentor. But when we discussed it, I realized that I did not have to write a diary entry, nor a literary masterpiece with a plot and a dastardly villain. I only needed to write a glorified index. The sole job of this paragraphed contents list was to explain briefly why every document was included. If it did that, it would succeed as an evaluative statement, be suitably reflective, and tie together my whole portfolio. And all in just two pages!

I had come to libraries in a very traditional way: a first degree, then a trainee year, followed by a Master's in Librarianship. At the start of the traineeship, I went to a formal talk with a lecturer from the nearby library school, and he was the first to hammer home the importance of Chartering as soon as possible – for the money, the career prospects and the contacts. I still remember my initial horror at the thought of yet more hurdles. But there was so much help at hand – and he was right. When I started work, I found that my library authority was very keen on putting all new recruits straight onto a training programme in order to see the wider professional context. This created a strong, supportive network which transferred very naturally into a Chartership support network. The obligatory workshop and mentor were arranged for us with no hassle, and all we then needed to do was prepare the portfolio. The bottom drawer of my desk became a deposit box and the documents, many more than I would ever use, piled up.

## Collating the evidence

By the time the drawer was overflowing, I needed a little guidance to help with the collating. CILIP's four assessment criteria, once I had thought about what they really meant, gave me the signposting I needed. But before I matched my documents to them, I needed to convince myself of the reasons that every particular piece of work was included. One of them demonstrated my teamwork skills, which have greatly improved since I started work. Another showed how I had applied my new knowledge to a specific problem which needed solving. If I could not persuade myself (and you know who they say is your harshest critic), then the document was rejected. If I could persuade myself, then the reason went into the evaluative statement.

I quickly realized that I would soon end up with a jumbled mess unless I gave the statement a tight structure. Having virtually memorized the four assessment criteria by this point, I used them to outline four clear and direct paragraphs. No introduction or conclusion, just the meat of the evidence. Now I had a framework I could use, along with those key sentences and phrases to slot in. The first word count was rather excessive, and it took some editing to remove repetitions and to shorten sentences to their snappiest and sharpest format. My mentor's proofreading was invaluable: someone else can often spot what your own eyes skim past. By the time I had pared it down to 1000 words, I definitely had an evaluative statement and not, to my relief, a diary.

## Selecting the evidence

Cross-referencing (putting numbers in brackets all over the place) should be easy. At least, if the documents stay where they are, it should. In reshuffling, removing and replacing documents I ended up renumbering them at least three times. Nonetheless, the process was a foolproof way of ensuring that I referred to every piece of evidence in the evaluative statement. As I struggled to include more than 25 items of evidence in the 1000 words, this actually made the statement an easy way of limiting the number of documents to include in the portfolio.

I had to make some tough decisions. My involvement in a local studies publication was surprisingly hard to tailor to meet the criteria. Without matching the criteria, it would have actually weakened the portfolio. Later I noticed that I was using two sets of meeting minutes, and I had selected them both for the same reason. Duplication is pointless, and one set had to go. It was not until I wrote the evaluative statement that these glitches really stood out. But, consequently, in the finished portfolio no page was wasted, and I had ensured that every document had really earned its right to be there.

## Conclusion: Giving shape to your career

Since I hit the ground running, having known about Chartership before I started work, I was able to complete my portfolio in a year. The process itself really focused my attention on my career and personal development. When I started job-hunting in the middle of it all, I found I had valuable information ready to hand: development needs and examples of good work are both prime interview material. Preparing for Chartership also stimulates a supportive network of people in the same position as yourself, either physically in your local area or virtually via discussion lists. These contacts may last for your entire career. It is hard to appreciate the journey when you feel overburdened and pressured. But it is worth it, and it is not just jumping through hoops. You are putting your career into shape by creating a portfolio. You will hone your strengths and address your weaknesses by doing some reflective writing. And you may as well use all those skills you developed when you last wrote in a diary.

## CASE STUDY 6.3
**Sue Westcott: Writing the personal statement for my Fellowship portfolio**

## What is Fellowship?

What does the word 'fellowship' conjure up in your mind? For me, as a childhood devotee of all things Tolkien, it meant a band of friends, with different strengths, weaknesses and personalities, hopes and dreams, on a long journey with a clear end in mind. There are difficulties to overcome, challenges to enjoy, and dragons and demons to be avoided, all made easier by the strength of your relationship with fellow travellers. My career has very much been like that and achievement of my Fellowship was no different. What my Fellowship also gave me was a wonderful way to reflect, be clear about my own role and decide how I wanted that journey to continue.

So, Fellowship, surely that is for 'Fellows'? For the great and the good? For those with national careers or experience based on academic excellence? Not for someone who still felt at the end of the first phase of her career who, although she had achieved a certain amount, felt that that had been through working with her colleagues, through doing her job and who certainly did not have the wealth of experience and achievements of some of her peers? Surely, if I applied for Fellowship I'd be found out. . . . Well, I'm living proof that that is not true – Fellowship is not the preserve of those rare, exalted few, looking towards a well-deserved retirement. It's something we should all consider when we have sufficient experience and achievement to demonstrate our professional experience since Chartership.

## Why Fellowship?

How did my journey begin? I was very fortunate in that my first post was in a government library which had a clear programme to work towards Chartership, and that my chief librarian was very supportive throughout that process and then insisted that I got on and submitted my Chartership, achieving it within two years of starting my first professional post. I remember the thrill of knowing that my professional body recognized my abilities. Years passed, I changed posts, learned new skills and got involved in CILIP (The Library Association as it was then) through my specialist interest group and then went on to be the Councillor for the group. All with good friends and colleagues supporting and encouraging me. A series of career development workshops made me realize that although I had clearly made considerable progress in my career I had no yardstick to measure this by and, being a rather goal-orientated individual, I began to look for a yardstick. Occasionally, someone would suggest Fellowship, but it would pass me idly by, on my mental 'to do' list, when I had time, when there weren't other things to do. Increasingly, however, it came up in conversation with three particular friends, and together we resolved to do something about it.

## Preparing the statement: Team work

Having committed, we were then faced with the prospect of actually applying, but having all promised each other, no one could really back out. We were all equally busy, all equally unsure where to start, and all trying to work out why we thought we should be Fellows. First we checked what we had to do by obtaining the CILIP guidance and making sure we all understood it. We got examples of key documents from CILIP's very helpful

Qualifications and Professional Development Department. We began to identify the evidence we wanted to base our applications on – much hunting around in old computer files, boxes of career documents, lofts, drawers at work and so on. We each drafted a CV and circulated it to one another and commented – identifying areas where someone hadn't expressed their achievements clearly enough, or where perhaps more detail was needed – as we knew that assessors who didn't know us, our work, or the sectors we'd worked in would be making the decision on our application.

The most intimidating requirement was the statement setting out why each of us thought we were worthy of CILIP's highest achievement. To support each other, we set one Saturday aside and spent the day at Maggie's. Each with our own space to work and no distractions we had no choice but to get on and put finger to laptop. Periodically we would re-group, be rewarded with cake and coffee, lunch, wine and nibbles, and would critically examine each other's documents and make suggestions for improvement in structure and content, and remind each other of the achievements we'd gained (and sometimes forgotten).

How on earth to start? That first sentence took me more effort than the rest of the statement put together. We all took different approaches but, generally speaking, we each identified two or three themes which would tie our evidence together and which fitted the criteria for Fellowship. In my case the focus was on knowledge and development of the government library sector, professional involvement in CILIP and work in the wider information management environment. The day passed into the evening and by dinner we'd each got a CV and a statement which only needed finer tuning. All of us pulled together our portfolios and off they went to CILIP shortly afterwards. The result was four very proud individuals at Members' Day in November.

## Conclusion

Three years on, what has it all meant? The process of writing my applications made me reflect on what I have enjoyed most and what I've got most satisfaction from in my career. I've used that to develop a very loose plan for moving forward and now have a new job, on the fringes of information management, where there is plenty of opportunity to try new things and learn new skills. I've spoken about Fellowship with enthusiasm to other colleagues who had achieved a lot but felt unworthy, several of whom as a result have gone on to achieve Fellowships too. It's also got me into better habits. I now keep my CV up to date, and keep a better archive and a list of achievements and professional development. I've always been an advocate of Revalidation, and so in the next year I will measure once again how far I have come professionally.

# 7

## Supporting evidence

### What is supporting evidence?

The supporting evidence is probably the largest part of your portfolio. You will have collected a great deal of evidence of your professional developmental activities over the qualifying period. The most important things to remember are that each piece of evidence should demonstrate that you meet the criteria for the relevant award, that each document should evidence the points made in your personal statement, and that you need to be able to evidence a variety of developmental activities over a period of time.

### Select your evidence

You will probably not need to include all the evidence you have collected; choose your evidence well. If you have used a matrix to record your developmental activities against the assessment criteria, as suggested earlier, you should find the whole process of choosing and sorting your evidence easier. Later in this chapter Ruth Wilkinson gives an example of how the matrix can be used in Chartership. The matrix should also help you to identify any gaps in your evidence. The aim is to choose items for your portfolio which are core to your application. There may be some of your documents which repeat the same point as others and can thus be omitted; for example, you don't need to include copies of all your PowerPoint presentations or all the information leaflets you have created. A sample of presentations, talks or flyers is sufficient. As Isabel

Hood (2006) says, 'portfolios become slimmer with experience in constructing them and length of professional practice'.

One of the most frequently asked questions at CILIP qualifications events is how much supporting material should be sent? The answer, predictably, is 'As much as is necessary'! For Certification you do not really need more than ten pieces of evidence. So be selective. There should be more supporting evidence for Chartership and Fellowship candidates, but again, quality is more important than quantity. For Revalidation, if you have done a lot of developmental activity, then the CPD log will give a full list and you can discuss your overall development based on the audit sheet and again be selective about the documents you include. My strong advice here is to seek individual guidance from your mentor or from the Candidate Support Officers in your area.

## Types of evidence

So what kind of evidence can you use? The answer is anything that shows your own professional development over the required period. There is no prescriptive list. All of us will have very different stories to tell of our own development and will choose the most appropriate documents to support that story. Common items include:

- evaluations of any training (in-house or external)
- information you have created for users
- reports
- published articles
- presentations
- performance reviews or appraisal records
- photographs of exhibitions
- minutes of meetings
- notes from conferences or visits
- web pages
- diaries
- blogs
- letters.

If you are a Chartership candidate you also need to choose materials which show that you understand the objectives of the organization you work for, and of the information services and products that the organization provides. But, very importantly, you also need to evaluate how those objectives are being met. This is a really good opportunity to include a piece of reflective writing. Don't just give the results of any surveys carried out; try to draw your own conclusions and perhaps even suggest ways to improve the service.

## Make your evidence relevant

You will need to have hard copies of your evidence even if the original is an e-document or on a website. The assessor may not have easy access to the internet. The important thing to remember is to make sure that the evidence is appropriate and shows that you meet the assessment criteria. The assessor needs to be able to understand what the evidence means. So, for example, only include organizational structure charts if they show where you fit in; only include minutes of meetings if they show your contributions; if including a report or article produced by a team, make sure it is clear how exactly you contributed to it; and don't send copies of every certificate you have if all they show is that you attended the course! You can annotate any documents you include if explaining their relevance a little more would be beneficial; it is an opportunity to show your evaluation and reflective skills. So, as you add your pieces of evidence to your file, write a note about the evidence to make it easier when you come to collate all the material and reflect further.

## Organize your evidence

You should try to be well organized as you start the whole process of putting together your portfolio, but for most of us that means keeping a big box of hard copy documents and an electronic file of any e-documents. If you are starting out with your Certification or Chartership registration you can be a little more organized from the very beginning. Use your information skills! Organize your documents into plastic wallets or folders under themes, for example, ICT training, reader development and information literacy or, if you prefer, use as headings the assessment criteria. Obviously some documents may well fit into more than one category, so make a cross-reference. This will also help you when you come to cross-reference your personal statement. I find box files really useful to help organize the material into broad categories. Doing this helped me to check that I had evidence for each criterion and also alerted me if there was too much or too little evidence.

## Reflect on your evidence

If you start in a methodical way at the beginning of the process, you can also get into good habits of reflection. Before you file your evidence, think about it and make some notes for yourself. For example, if it is a certificate of training, evaluate the training, and comment on how you will apply the new skills acquired and knowledge learned; this will be useful when you come to review the evidence and write your personal statement. It is so much easier to make a note immediately after the event, and then reflect later on the longer-term outcomes. If you have visited another information service, record your opinions of that service and make a note of anything you could use in your own workplace. If you are required to write a report on any conference or presentation you attend, keep a copy of it – if not required for work, try doing it for yourself! If you have given a presentation or have led a training event, make sure you evaluate it and write up what went well and what could have been better. Become a reflective practitioner. It may seem strange at first, making notes for yourself about what you do at work, but gradually it will become second nature.

If you are an experienced practitioner you may already have a great deal of evidence which you will need to sort through and arrange into some form of logical sequence. This is probably more difficult than starting off in an organized way. You may, like me, discover that some of the evidence has disappeared into the ether. If you are applying for Certification, Chartership or Fellowship after more than five years, you need to concentrate on the last two to three, although, for Fellowship, evidence of achievement throughout your whole career is important. Use your annotated CV to evidence your professional development before the period you are concentrating on. You can include lists of courses and conferences attended and can annotate those lists with some reflective comments. Then, using the appropriate matrix for your qualification, try to map your developmental activities and the evidence against the criteria.

The approach to presenting the evidence for Revalidation is similar. You have the ongoing CPD log and should be using the audit sheet to help you reflect on the learned outcomes of your training and development. Some of you will have many examples of developmental activities. The CPD log will list them all, but you can use the audit sheet to start to cluster the many activities into categories. In this way you can reflect on your overall learning.

As a mentor one of the most useful things I have found is to ask my mentees to produce a contents list of the evidence they are going to submit. This makes you think about the choice of evidence and its organization. Producing the contents list for another person ensures that the structure makes sense to someone else. Quite often we are too close to our own portfolio to review its structure critically.

## Letters of support

A letter of support is a required element of the portfolio for Certification, Fellowship and Revalidation. The letter should be from the person who can best endorse your suitability for the qualification. There is no template for letters of support but there are guidelines on the CILIP website. Once you have decided whom to ask, you should ask them as promptly as possible, make sure they understand what is required and let them have a copy of the guidelines and the assessment criteria. Then, when you have a final draft of your personal statement, let them have a copy, and, if impractical to show them the whole of the rest of the portfolio, at least the contents list. Always give them a deadline, and if you do not hear from them, do get back in touch. Letters of support should normally be from Chartered Members of CILIP; however, for some information practitioners who are solo workers, a letter from your line manager should also be included if this is the most appropriate person to comment on your development.

For Chartership, evidence of your participation in the mentoring scheme is required and this could be in the form of a letter from your mentor, or your diary of meetings and actions.

For Revalidation and Certification only one letter is required, but for Fellowship it is normal to include several. How many you decide to include will very much depend on the application you are making. For some Fellowship applicants, much of the evidence will be in published books and articles; for others letters of support from senior colleagues will be important. When I applied for my Fellowship I felt that much of the evidence I needed was in people, so I asked colleagues at the university, former students and CILIP colleagues in the North East. Remember that one of the letters of support should come from another Chartered Member or Fellow of CILIP.

## Organizing the evidence

Once you have decided on what evidence you are going to include you should decide how you will organize it so that the assessor can easily look from the personal statement to the appropriate evidence. Always remember that you know how everything fits together, but that you are presenting the portfolio to other Chartered Members who do not know you or where you work. Make it easy for the assessors to find the information they need.

### Hints and tips

- ☞ Start collecting your evidence as soon as you can.
- ☞ Annotate the evidence where appropriate.
- ☞ Organize evidence into broad categories.
- ☞ Use a matrix to map evidence against criteria.
- ☞ Review and revise your evidence 'box' regularly so you can ensure you have all the evidence you need.

☞ Select specific evidence needed to meet the assessment criteria.
☞ Compile a contents list.
☞ Avoid repetition and duplication.
☞ Remember quality not quantity.

CASE STUDY 7.1
**Ruth Wilkinson: Supporting evidence for my Chartership portfolio**

On commencing my role as Information Specialist at NBS (National Building Specification) I became a Member of CILIP and went along to a Chartership workshop. We carried out a series of exercises that helped me to reflect on the value and purpose of training. I used the results of these exercises to assess where I needed further training and discussed this with my manager at my next performance review.

A fairly new graduate, I needed to complete the year of professional experience before applying. During this year my training objectives were to gain more construction-industry-orientated knowledge to enable me to understand the information needs of my client group. I also needed to refresh my information skills and become more proficient at using Microsoft Access. This was achieved by attending a number of courses, visits and knowledge-sharing seminars, professional reading, a conference and activities within my team.

## Building evidence

In some cases I was asked to take notes and distribute them for the benefit of the rest of the information services team. This was useful evidence to support event handouts and certificates of attendance; I began to organize a folder containing material from each event I had attended. I also wrote a personal reflection after each event, which highlighted the value of the training and its relevance to my personal and professional development.

I registered under the new Chartership regulations in May 2006, along with three other members of my team. It made sense for us all to try to get the same mentor and help each other through the process. The first meeting with our mentor was to discuss the personal and professional development plan and material for evidence. We had prepared a list of questions, and after the meeting my understanding was that many types of evidence could be used so long as they met the criteria of assessment. I also planned to use evidence obtained prior to registration, as it was relevant to my development. Our mentor suggested that we use a table containing the criteria of assessment as headings, and then enter our activities to see how they met the criteria. She called this a Chartership matrix (see Figure 7.1). I found this a very worthwhile exercise, as it defined the importance of the training and displayed patterns of development.

## Reviewing professional evidence

I spent the next month working on my CV and PPDP. My training requirements are discussed every six months at performance reviews and, although training was driven by work activities, my employer encouraged me to attend events that would broaden my knowledge within the library profession. The records of my performance reviews provided a good framework for the PPDP. I also tried to include as much information as possible on my CV; I cross-referenced to it from my personal statement. This was a good way of keeping the word count down and providing a clear picture of skills gained and achievements to date.

I chose to revisit the notes from the Chartership workshop to try to define the skills I needed to develop through training. I carried out a SWOT analysis and gave it to three people who knew me well to make comments. I also did a skills audit (Figure 7.2), using skills mentioned in the CILIP Body of Professional Knowledge. I found both of these exercises interesting; they illustrated my strengths and weaknesses, which helped me set objectives for my PPDP and performance reviews.

When completing the Chartership matrix I returned to my original notes from courses attended. In some cases I had found the course interesting but not that useful. As time passed my views changed and I was able to apply some of the skills or knowledge gained to my work activities. This has taught me to be more open minded about training opportunities and to try to enhance my knowledge of the profession outside my work activities.

| Activity | Criterion 1 | Criterion 2 | Criterion 3 | Criterion 4 | Evidence |
|---|---|---|---|---|---|
| | Ability to reflect critically on personal performance and to evaluate service performance | Active commitment to CPD | Ability to analyse personal and professional development with reference to experiential and developmental activities | Breadth of knowledge and understanding of the wider professional context. | |
| Aardvark Training in-house at NBS. | Evaluate service performance through testing of products and reporting bugs and errors through the Aardvark system. | Yes. | Needed to undertake this training to be able to take part in product testing on a regular basis. | No. | |
| Visit to Dublin. March 2005. | Visiting customers allowed me to evaluate service performance. | Not especially. | Identified areas of weakness in the product and will work to improve these. I have gained more of an understanding of Irish computer information systems (CIS) needs. | Broadened knowledge of specialist subject area. | E-mail. Notes taken on visit. |
| Designing classification schemes for effective records management – CILIP London. 26/04/2005. | Needed to design a new classification scheme for the FM product and I lacked knowledge of doing so. | Yes, it built on what I learnt at university. | Was able to put different ways of classifying documents into the context of my work at NBS. | Yes, the exercises carried out highlighted other roles people have within the profession. | Certificate of attendance. Training evaluation form. Completed exercises. List of attendees. |
| Chartership Workshop. 06/06/2005. | Reviewing recent skills attained. | Preparation for the Chartership process. | Yes, carried out a series of activities to demonstrate skills obtained to date and areas of weakness. | Yes, was able to talk to others who have different roles within the profession. | Certificate of attendance. Completed exercises (very useful). List of attendees. |
| TASI Workshop – Digital rights management. 16/06/2005. | Not especially. | Yes. | Yes could use exercises to put theory into context of my work at NBS. | Yes, most of the attendees worked in academic libraries and needed to digitize image collections. | Certificate of attendance. Completed exercises. Training evaluation form. |

**Figure 7.1** Chartership matrix

(continued on next page)

| Activity | Criterion 1 | Criterion 2 | Criterion 3 | Criterion 4 | Evidence |
|---|---|---|---|---|---|
| | *Ability to reflect critically on personal performance and to evaluate service performance* | *Active commitment to CPD* | *Ability to analyse personal and professional development with reference to experiential and developmental activities* | *Breadth of knowledge and understanding of the wider professional context.* | |
| Architecture Week 2005. | Not especially. | Not especially. | Gave me a little more insight into the construction industry. | Not especially. | Brochure and notes or information collected from visits. |
| ARCLIB conference Dublin 13. 15/07/2005. | Not especially but did get the chance to talk to some CIS customers about the content of the product. | Yes. | Got a bit more of an insight into the information needs of some of our academic users (most of the attendees were from academic libraries). This will be useful when selecting documents. | Yes lots of opportunities to network. | Notes. Conference programme of events. Training evaluation form. Performance review. |
| Access Training in-house 16–17/11/ 2005. | Yes. | Yes. | Yes, I am now able to do queries and reports and can be part of the index production rota. | Not especially. | Certificate of attendance. Training evaluation form. Performance review. |
| BIFM Conference – North region. 18/11/2005. | Was able to evaluate FM product after gaining an insight into information needs of Facilities Managers. | Yes, it broadened my knowledge in specialist subject areas. | Enhanced specialist subject knowledge that will contribute to work activities. | More of an understanding of the FM industry. | Training evaluation form. Conference notes. |
| The Facilities Show – Birmingham. 09/05/2005. | It was reassuring to see we include relevant subjects and material in the facilities management product. It outlined new legislation coming up to include. | Yes, it broadened my knowledge in specialist subject areas by attending the seminars. | Expanded my knowledge of FM subjects in order to develop the management supplement to the product. | More of an understanding of the FM industry. | Conference notes. Training evaluation form. |

**Figure 7.1** *(Continued)* Chartership matrix

*(continued on next page)*

| Activity | Criterion 1 | Criterion 2 | Criterion 3 | Criterion 4 | Evidence |
|---|---|---|---|---|---|
| | Ability to reflect critically on personal performance and to evaluate service performance | Active commitment to CPD | Ability to analyse personal and professional development with reference to experiential and developmental activities | Breadth of knowledge and understanding of the wider professional context. | |
| Visit to Dublin. 31/05/2006. | Points were raised about improvements that could be made to Irish CIS. | Not especially. | No | Not especially. | E-mail. Notes taken during visit. |
| Visit to Seven Stories Centre for Children's Books. 13/06/2006. | No. | Yes. | No. | Yes, a look into the different ways that information can be stored and presented in a variety of formats to appeal to a wide audience. | Photo. Brochure. Notes taken. |
| Visit to RIBA Library London. 06/07/2006. | Yes. | Yes. | Yes, it gave me an understanding of RIBA Enterprises in the wider context and a sense of the importance of the work we do at NBS on the CIS products. | Yes, I gained an understanding into what other roles people carry out in the same organization. Although very different you can see some similarities. | Brochure. Notes taken. Photo. |
| Visit to the British Library. 06/07/2006. | Not especially. | Yes. | Not especially. | Yes. Combined with article in the *Director* and others alike you can see the way forward for libraries and information centres in the 21st century. | Notes taken. Publications from the British Library. Article in the *Director* – 'Extending shelf life'. |

**Figure 7.1** *(Continued)* Chartership matrix

*(continued on next page)*

| Activity | Criterion 1 | Criterion 2 | Criterion 3 | Criterion 4 | Evidence |
|---|---|---|---|---|---|
| | *Ability to reflect critically on personal performance and to evaluate service performance* | *Active commitment to CPD* | *Ability to analyse personal and professional development with reference to experiential and developmental activities* | *Breadth of knowledge and understanding of the wider professional context.* | |
| NBS IKSS Seminars Jan 05–May 06. | Yes, most of these evaluated service performance. | Yes, subjects vary but I've only attended those which are relevant to my role or profession. | Yes. | Yes, keeps me up-to-date with changes in web design, information management and the construction industry's information need. | Schedule Notes taken/PPT slides. |
| BIFM Q&A session and Networking Event. | Able to assess whether the service satisfies information needs in specific subject areas. | Not especially; it was aimed at Facilities Managers. | Not especially. | More of an understanding of FM subject areas. | Notes taken. |
| Core Skills of Facilities Management – Hawksmere Consultancy. Manchester. | Was able to use the information given to assess service performance. | Yes. | Gained more of an understanding of the different activities in facilities management. | Yes, more understanding of subject areas and the roles of an FM. | Certificate. |
| NBS. Understanding the Construction Industry. | To be completed over the next six months. | | | | |
| CILIP. Abstracting with Confidence. | Yes, able to assess my abstracting skills and define where improvement is needed. | Yes. | Yes, could put this into the context of my role. | Yes, I could apply these new skills to another library and information role. | Certificate. |

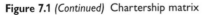

**Figure 7.1** *(Continued)* Chartership matrix

## Drafting my statements

I agreed with my mentor to try to get a draft personal and evaluative statement written by the end of August. This proved difficult to begin with, so

I used the Chartership matrix and PPDP to identify areas of development and material to support it. I received feedback on my statement and was then asked to provide a draft contents page. I felt this exercise really clarified what evidence to include and gave me a framework of what my portfolio would contain. I decided to split the evidence into five sections: organizational context, personal performance, service performance, commitment to continuing professional development and professional knowledge.

Using the draft contents page I began to build a rough portfolio. This highlighted areas where I needed to provide more evidence and amend my personal statement. I had another meeting with my mentor in October, when we went through my draft portfolio. In essence she was satisfied that I was on the right track and that I just needed to write it all up. We agreed that I would try to submit before the end of 2006. During this time I continued to attend events and participate in activities that would contribute to the portfolio. I began to take charge of my personal and professional development.

Finally, I submitted my portfolio in January 2007. I was lucky to have the support of a good mentor and work colleagues; I also joined an informal

Subject knowledge       Information dissemination
     **Document processing**      Indexing
     **Communication**
**Understanding user information need**      Document construction
     **Metadata**      **Content analysis**      Abstracting
**Content evaluation**      **Secondary processing**      **Document selection**
     Document storage      Cataloguing      **Classification**
Document preservation      Records management   Data mining
     **Information retrieval**      Website and portal design
**Database maintenance**      Information service moderation
**Information service analysis**   Information ethics      **Customer service**
User behaviour      Information regulations    **Intellectual property**
     Accessibility      **Computer literacy**      **Interpersonal skills**
Management skills    Marketing    Training    Mentoring    **Research**

**Note**
I have gained some skills in abstracting and records management but feel that there is still room for improvement in these areas. This exercise was very useful prior to my annual performance review where I have the opportunity to request training needs and ensure that development is in areas where I am weak.

**Figure 7.2** Skills Audit – 1 August 2006 (based on CDG worksheet)

Chartership group in my area which met every few months and had an e-mail forum. Once I was clear as to what was required, I enjoyed putting the portfolio together and I feel it has given me a sense of achievement and a vision for the future.

The skills shown in Figure 7.2 have been taken from the CILIP Body of Professional Knowledge. Those in bold indicate competent skills gained from career at NBS to date.

## CASE STUDY 7.2
### Ayub Khan: Supporting evidence for my Fellowship portfolio

I always thought that Fellowship was for those Members who were near to retirement and had written and published numerous publications of an academic nature. I was wrong; it is an award for all stages of your career so long as you meet the criteria. I was one of the youngest Members to put in an application for Fellowship and I must confess that I raised a few eyebrows from certain colleagues when I told them that I was working on my application.

Fellowship is within the grasp of any Member of CILIP, and those who achieve it should find it of value in demonstrating their continuing professional development to employers, as I have. I found it a useful experience in consolidating my professional progress to date, reflecting on what I had achieved and perhaps where I wanted to go next in my career.

Before applying, I took advice from the Qualifications and Professional Development Department at CILIP, who were very helpful and gave me some pointers to think about when putting my portfolio together. They impressed upon me that I should read the regulations very carefully and pay particular attention to the criteria for admission to the register of Fellows.

I also contacted a couple of colleagues who had already been through the Fellowship experience and sought their advice on how they had gone about compiling their application. I was surprised at how little was published on this. There was a significant amount of information about Chartering and training events on how best to go about submitting a Chartership application, but Fellowship was surprisingly poorly covered in the literature.

Again, my colleagues who had gone through Fellowship themselves told me to pay particular attention to the assessment criteria and to the need to demonstrate the following in my application:

- evidence of substantial achievement in professional practice
- evidence of significant contribution to all or part of the profession
- evidence of active commitment to continuing professional development.

The criteria for the award of Fellowship are defined in terms of the enhancement of your intellectual and professional skills and the contribution you have made to the development of the profession. I had been particularly active in the Career Development Group from a very early stage and had progressed to President of the Group (one of the largest special interest groups in CILIP) and was instrumental in setting up the new Diversity Group, which I drew on in my application for Fellowship. When I looked into Fellowship I soon found out that Fellowship candidates had extremely varied experience and that the Chartership Board (which assesses the applications) is asked to consider a wide range of evidence, so this also influenced the evidence that I presented in my application.

## Sorting and sifting the evidence

The main bulk of my application consisted of a portfolio, which I divided into sections relating to the criteria outlined in the Fellowship handbook. I started to work on my portfolio early on and invested in a sturdy ring binder and plenty of plastic wallets. Over the years I had assembled a lot of paper which provided evidence of CPD, involvement in professional activities and contributions to publications and conferences. It was fortuitous that I was compiling my portfolio at the same time as I was having an office sort-out and came across all manner of items I had forgotten about, some dating back 15 years, when I was a student rep on the Local Youth Libraries Group.

The hardest part of the whole process was sifting through the mountain of paper I had accumulated over the years and deciding what to include and, much harder, what not to include. I did not want my application to seem as if I had not been selective about the material and I only wanted items to feature that were relevant and that illustrated the types of activities I had been involved in.

I numbered each piece of evidence very clearly and wrote short annotations to provide the assessors with the context as to why I had included this particular piece of evidence and how it linked with the criteria. My NVQ assessors' training was very useful in this respect. I also included a very comprehensive contents page outlining the evidence presented and the document numbers of the evidence.

You can include any papers, certificates, presentations and DVD material which you have relating to the type of work in your portfolio. A well presented portfolio will highlight your organizational skills as well as your written communication skills. I tried to demonstrate originality in my portfolio along with indicating the breadth and depth of work I have undertaken and the technical competency which the Assessment Panel are looking for. I organized my portfolio into specific sections addressing selected skills/competencies (see below).

## My evidence categories

The type of documentary or other evidence you present can be any material you believe relevant to your personal statement. I included the following:

- research, which I undertook on particular projects during my career, including work on a new library project I was working on at the time
- published material – sample copies of articles I had published in the professional literature and PowerPoint presentations I had given
- evidence of practical professional achievement of any kind such as my NVQ assessor's Certification, awards, reports and papers I was particularly proud of
- accounts of professional work with supporting evidence, including committee meeting minutes, strategies and policy papers I had produced and conferences that I had organized or attended.

I tried to include projects that I'd worked on in my current job or within the last few years for currency, although for some evidence I drew on a longer period.

## Evaluating your evidence

Remember that it is important to not be descriptive but to be evaluative. For example, I attended Umbrella, so said, 'I attended the Umbrella conference in Hatfield and found it really useful to attend the seminars and meet colleagues from other sectors. I learnt the frustrations that staff are experiencing in the HE [higher education] sector, concerning access to electronic resources. I realize that public library staff may have similar issues if the same ethos is adopted.'

Remember that the technical capabilities of the assessors are going to vary widely vary. Always give an alternative access option for all items that you have encoded using proprietary software (for example, PowerPoint, Adobe PDF, and RealAudio).

## Meeting the assessment criteria

What not to include – don't include things that do not relate to the criteria that the Assessment Panel are looking for. As an NVQ assessor myself, I did get frustrated with the weight of evidence that candidates submitted which was not relevant.

Key points for your portfolio should be:

- address the criteria
- look for proof to demonstrate competency
- be ruthless in what you exclude
- pay attention to detail and presentation.

I ensured that in my application I demonstrated the attributes mentioned in the criteria and included evidence of my CPD activities over the past four to five years, together with conference papers and talks I had given at local, national and international conferences.

## The assessment

Once I had completed my application and read it through very carefully (for spelling and grammar errors, etc.), I had done all I could and my fate was in the hands of the Chartership Board who would assess my application. The Board has a total membership of 20. All are Chartered Members or Fellows. A number of those appointed have had experience of teaching at postgraduate level and/or of examining at all levels, including research degrees. The Board also appoints two external examiners to ensure that the Board complies with its regulations and procedures. With this information in mind, I was assured that my application would be treated professionally and fairly. I was pleased that my application would be assessed by my peers and other Fellows. It took me approximately three to four months to complete my submission. It seemed a long wait to hear from the Board. Finally, the assessment of my application was completed and it was positive – I was a Fellow!

## The benefits of Fellowship

Fellowship has helped me with my career progression, enhancing my standing with other colleagues, and has provided me with the personal satisfaction of achievement. One further advantage of receiving my Fellowship award is that the Open University Validation Service (OUVS) has agreed to award 75 Master's level credits for successful completion of Fellowship. The credit can be used in the OUVS Credit Accumulation and Transfer Scheme (CATS), and can be very beneficial to Chartered Fellows who may wish to pursue a higher degree, as it can be used towards obtaining qualifications in a number of disciplines, not just Library and Information Studies, which is a temping offer and recognizes the high standard of this award within the academic environment and outside of the sector.

The application process genuinely helped me to reflect on and evaluate my achievements and lessons learned during my career so far and, perhaps more importantly, in assessing future opportunities and direction for my career path.

It was great if not a little nerve-racking to receive the award (the highest in the profession!) at Members' Day (with the whole of the Presidential team also receiving their Fellowship awards too) in front of friends, colleagues and peers all celebrating and recognizing achievement within the profession. I have my Fellowship certificate hanging on the wall in my office in Warwickshire (adjacent to my Chartership certificate). I am immensely proud of it, and take pride in showing off this accolade to colleagues both within and outside of the library sector.

If I can achieve Fellowship, so can you!

## Appendix: Portfolio contents

Curriculum vitae

Supporting statement for Fellowship

Supporting statement from colleagues

*Section one*

*'Have the ability to carry out demanding work.'*

| Evidence 1 | Articles on the new Library of Birmingham. |
| Evidence 2 | Prospectus – setting out a vision for a library of the future; was responsible for final editing of this document. |
| Evidence 3 | Promotional and publicity material for new library project, which I was tasked to produce. |
| Evidence 4 | Birmingham Libraries newsletter – interview about why a new library was needed. |
| Evidence 5 | Joint author of an article in *Update* – setting out the vision for a new library – sharing our thinking with the wider profession. |
| Evidence 6 | Article based on a talk at Umbrella exploring the library of the future. |
| Evidence 7 | City Council staff newsletter – skills learned/my role in library project. |
| Evidence 8 | Factsheets I produced detailing aspects of the project – frequently asked questions from the public. |
| Evidence 9 | Report on the market research for the new library, which I presented to the Library of Birmingham Steering Group. |
| Evidence 10 | Article for CILIP West Midlands Branch newsletter, reporting on a new Cabe publication on new libraries. |

*Section two*

'*Have the ability to handle complex professional issues.*'

Evidence 11     Article for *LA Record* – 'Stephen Lawrence Inquiry: implication for libraries'.

Evidence 12     Report back from Black Contribution to British Librarianship Conference.

Evidence 13     Article on a project in Birmingham (Under 5s) that I was involved with regarding social inclusion.

Evidence 14     Published article about the challenges of race equality in libraries.

Evidence 15     Write-up from a presentation on the subject of social exclusion and the role of libraries.

Evidence 16     Joint article looking at extremism on the internet, which was published in 2000 when this was a new area of public concern in libraries.

Evidence 17     Write-up on a conference which I attended regarding race and libraries.

Evidence 18     Letter nominating for Diversity Award.

Evidence 19     Certificate – highly commended, for personal achievement award, CILIP.

Evidence 20     Diversity Group Newsletter featuring award winners.

Evidence 21     PowerPoint slides on a talk to Youth Libraries Group (YLG) on the theme of social inclusion and special needs.

*Section three*

'*Are contributing to the profession in general or in a specific context.*'

Evidence 22     Interview (profile), which was featured in *Update*, with the editor of *Update*.

Evidence 23     Brochure produced by The LA (now CILIP) profiling individuals (including me) working in different sectors. Used as a tool in career fairs, etc.

Evidence 24     Letter from John Dolan (my manager) concerning involvement with the wider profession.

Evidence 25     Career Development Group – 'Meet the President' article, including themes for the year.

Evidence 26     Extract from the Umbrella programme 2003 – talk 'The changing library – moving from transactional to being transformational'.

Evidence 27     Letter from Paul Hamlyn Foundation asking me to participate in a discussion about the foundation's future grant-making programme.

Evidence 28     Pages from the British Council's website – featuring the Knowledge and Advisory Committee of which I am a member.

Evidence 29     British Council's 2010 strategy – which I contributed to as a KIAC (Knowledge and Information Advisory Committee) member.

Evidence 30     Committee report presented to Leisure Services Committee informing them on my award of a Library Association Centenary medal.

Evidence 31     Picture at the awards ceremony with the HRH the Princess Royal, British Library.

Evidence 32     Report to my employer for authorization to participate in 66th IFLA General Conference in Jerusalem, 2000, as a speaker.

Evidence 33     Report on 66th IFLA General Conference, Jerusalem, 2000 – which I co-wrote with Alison Minns.

Evidence 34     Article published in LA Record promoting IFLA and the 2002 Glasgow conference.

Evidence 35     Promotional material/announcements for Glasgow 2002, to which I contributed, and an e-mail discussion as part of the working party I served on.

Evidence 36     Letter from British Council (Athens) asking me to participate as a speaker in a Greek librarians' conference.

Evidence 37     PowerPoint slides (and notes) I used for the presentation at the above conference on the theme of social inclusion – promoting UK best practice.

Evidence 38     Programme for the Library and Information Conference Wales 2004 – was invited to speak at this conference.

Evidence 39    Public Libraries Group Spring Conference programme –
               details about my participation as a speaker at this
               important conference.
Evidence 40    Presentation handouts for the above conference, which
               demonstrate my thinking behind a new generation of library
               buildings and staff roles for the future.

## Section four

*'Are developing your professional knowledge.'*

Evidence 41    Table detailing my training and development activities.
Evidence 42    Article on homework support and out-of-hours learning and
               how this links with wider educational goals.
Evidence 43    Issue of *Impact*, Career Development Group (CDG) journal,
               and my introductory notes to the CDG national conference
               – Skills for the Future, which I attended and participated in.
Evidence 44    International issue of *Impact*, which I edited and which
               features a 'Study Tour' I organized and participated in to
               extend my professional knowledge.
Evidence 45    Programme for a conference organized by the British
               Council for information mangers from across Europe – I
               was asked to participate and speak at the conference on
               the theme of UK information sector perspectives.
Evidence 46    E-mail from the Laser Foundation asking me to participate
               in a 'Future of the Public Library Think Tank'.
Evidence 47    Notes from the above 'Think Tank' meeting in which I
               participated.

## Section five

*'Are maintaining and enhancing your professional competencies.'*

Evidence 48    Copy of Associate certificate awarded in 1995.
Evidence 49    Write-up from the Anglo-Scandinavian Public Libraries
               conference and study tour in Finland, which I attended.
Evidence 50    Programme of an event which I attended to encourage

greater partnership between libraries in the West Midlands and the British Library.

Evidence 51   Certificates for achieving the NVQ assessors award.

Evidence 52   Certificate of attendance for a research skills course I attended.

Evidence 53   Certificate for successfully completing my New Opportunities Fund (NOF)-funded ICT training programme for public library staff.

Evidence 54   Learning Line certificate for completing digital image training programme.

Evidence 55   Course programme for the ICT training programme (for library staff, including senior managers) which I tutored.

Evidence 56   Extracts from virtual conference website – which I tutored (12-week course). This included discussion topics on complex issues within the library and information field.

Evidence 57   Report on visits to libraries in the East End of London, lessons learned.

Evidence 58   Programme and notes from a seminar I attended 'Learning on-line'. This seminar was part of a programme of seminars I attended on strategic leadership.

Evidence 59   CDG National Conference programme which I attended.

Evidence 60   Flyer for an Information Services Group event – 'Building Virtual Communities' at which I was invited to speak.

Evidence 61   Presentation slides for my talk at the above event.

Evidence 62   Programme for a seminar I attended – 'Role of ICT in the future'.

Evidence 63   Programme for the CILIP East of England Branch annual event; I was asked to speak and participate during the day.

Evidence 64   Slides on the theme of 'Project Management' which I used for the talk at the above event.

## Where to start?

I started off by downloading all the templates and filling in the easy bits (name, Membership number, and so forth) to give myself a sense of having done something. I had thought that I might start by gathering evidence but soon rejected this idea, partly because I had changed jobs and, although I thought I had saved things, the things which I had saved were so mundane that they wouldn't add much to my portfolio. I also felt that it would be best not to have too much evidence but to make it really clear in my portfolio that I met the criteria. My view is very much that the best 'evidence' is in the evaluation of learning and its application.

CPD takes place through a wide range of activities – courses and conferences, yes, but also, and often more significantly, work-based experiences. The learning gained from the full range of activities needs to be clearly demonstrated in the application. There may be courses which demand and develop a high level of reflection and evaluation and it may be appropriate to include the certificate for such a course but otherwise my own view is that putting a certificate of attendance into the evidence part of the portfolio is largely superfluous – yes, it says that you were there, but it doesn't show what you learned (or indeed whether you learned anything!) and how you applied the learning.

I then moved on to the CPD log. This is simply a chronological list of activities undertaken during the period of Revalidation. Normally it should be done and submitted on an annual basis. I pulled mine together and found myself listing events that I had attended or delivered rather than reflecting on, and evaluating, my development. I moved on to the CPD audit sheet and immediately felt that this was the tool to move me forward!

## CPD audit sheet to the rescue

The CPD audit sheet is not mandatory and does not have to be included in the portfolio but, for me, it was the single most useful template as it really makes you reflect on what has been learned from an activity and how you applied the learning. If it is used and included in the portfolio it will be assessed along with everything else. I copied across the activities listed on my CPD log and I reflected on the key aspects of my development over the past three to four years. Many of these came from work-based experiences, for example, merger discussions, staff management, involvement in working groups/committees, and working with overseas colleagues. I started to include these in the CPD audit sheet and, almost instinctively, started to group developmental activities into 'themes' – for example, management, quality review and assessment. This tidied it up no end and gave me a 'shape' on which to base the personal statement.

Before I started on the personal statement, and to help me feel sure that I had included everything in the CPD audit sheet, I looked at my CV. I listed my qualifications and then moved on to employment, concentrating on the period of Revalidation by indicating achievements in the two posts which I had held during that period. I listed my wider professional activity, conference inputs and publications during the period of Revalidation. The end result was four sides of A4, focusing on the period of Revalidation and adding to the other items in my portfolio.

The final version of my CPD audit sheet was ten A4 sheets – probably a bit excessive but very much a demonstration of reflection on, and critical evaluation of, my learning from a range of training and development activities (Criterion 1), of my increased competence in a range of professional and management skills developed through professional practice (Criterion 2), and giving evidence of continuous professional development through reading, participation in professional affairs, and contribution to or attendance at courses/conferences and so on (Criterion 3).

## Personal statement and evidence

I then moved on to the personal statement. The work which I had done on the CPD audit sheet and my CV had helped me to identify what I saw as the key developmental activities during the period of Revalidation. Out of six activities listed in the first part of the personal statement template, only one was a training event. The others were work-based or professional activities which I reflected on and evaluated the learning gained and its application in my work and career. As far as possible I did not duplicate what was already included elsewhere in my application, rather, I expanded on things. In the summary section of the personal statement I summarized my development under the themes already identified in the CPD audit sheet, incorporating evaluation of the application of learning from the range of activities listed in the CPD log and the CPD audit sheet. Because of what was already in my CV and CPD audit sheet, I found it easy to stay within the word and length limit of the personal statement.

The remaining element was the evidence. Much of my learning and development had already been evidenced in the CPD audit sheet and in the personal statement, so I selected just seven items of evidence to support my application. I drew these from the themes which had already appeared in my application and took care to use materials which added to, rather than padded, my portfolio. They included my current job description, a quality document which I had produced, an extract from a conference report, training materials which I had developed for two key training events, an extract from a publication which I had co-edited and the letter of appointment to CILIP Chartership Board. There were lots of other things which I could have included but I chose the ones which fitted best with my overall application. I then went back to my CV and personal statement to include cross-references to the evidence section of the portfolio.

Once I had pulled together my application I shared it with my line manager in order that her supporting letter might reinforce what I had included.

## How did I present it all?

Having been an assessor, and having trained assessors, I was conscious of the need to present my portfolio in a way which facilitated its assessment against the criteria. The Revalidation scheme handbook indicates the mandatory elements of the portfolio . . . so why not put them into the portfolio in the order in which they appear? I produced a title page and a contents page to guide the assessors. I arranged the first copy as I intended to submit it, then carried out a 'self-assessment' against the Revalidation assessment form (on the CILIP web page for Revalidation) to check that I had demonstrated clearly that I met the criteria. I made four copies of everything (three to submit and one for myself) and put each copy into a clip file, clearly labelled with my name, Membership number and period of Revalidation.

## How much time did it all take?

Don't get the idea that I did all of this overnight – that could have been the case if I had acted immediately on my intentions! It was a few months in the 'meaning to do it' phase; however, once I set my mind to it and set a target submission date, the time spent totalled around three days:

'Thinking time' = 5 hours
Refocusing my CV = 2 hours
CPD log and CPD audit sheet = 5 hours
Personal statement = 2 hours
Selection of evidence = 1 hour
'Self-assessment' = 1 hour
Copying/printing/arranging in files = 4 hours
Checking everything = 2 hours
Checking everything again = 1 hour.

OK, because of my job in the CILIP Qualifications and Professional Development Department, I should understand the qualifications and their requirements. Nevertheless, the skills used were those acquired and honed in professional practice – namely, reflection, evaluation, communication, presentation, and so forth. If anything, I spent longer on my application simply because it would have been too embarrassing to submit a less-than-good portfolio.

## How long did I wait for a result?

Because I was revalidating my Fellowship, my application had to be assessed by the Chartership Board rather than by a CILIP Assessment Panel. I submitted in late August and my application was accepted by the

Chartership Board at its November meeting. As a former member of the Chartership Board I found this nerve-racking and experienced several 'crises of confidence'!

## How will I approach it next time?

My view is that Revalidation and performance appraisal have significant synergies, and I intend to kill two birds with one stone by drawing on my reflection and evaluation for both purposes. In many ways Revalidation is 'performance appraisal plus' with the 'plus' being the focus on personal professional development in a wider sense than job-specific development. Both Revalidation and performance appraisal require us to reflect on developmental activities, to evaluate learning and its application, to identify what has gone well/less well and evaluate the factors in this to identify what measures can be taken to maintain and improve performance. The thing that is missing from Revalidation is the requirement to draw up a development plan identifying developmental needs and ways of meeting them. However, there is no reason why this couldn't be done as part of a Revalidation portfolio – it would certainly demonstrate commitment to CPD and an ability to critically evaluate personal learning needs and outcomes.

There is an expectation that Revalidation is an ongoing process, with candidates submitting a CPD log each year and a full portfolio every three years. I intend to do this, but also to keep my own file on an ongoing basis, updating it at intervals when I reflect on my developmental activities. As I work in an organization which has appraisal twice yearly, this should be achievable.

# 8

# The final steps

Gathering all your documentation and drafting your personal statement will take time but there will come a point where you have to decide that you are ready to submit. I feel it is really important to set yourself a target date for submission, as it is very tempting just to continue compiling information and rewriting sections. Nothing sharpens the mind like a definite date for submitting.

As you reach the final steps in building your portfolio you need to remember four important questions:

1 Have you got all the required elements of your portfolio?
2 Is the structure and layout of your portfolio clear and is the portfolio presented well for the assessors?
3 Have you done a final check against the assessment criteria?
4 Have you proofread your portfolio or, preferably, got someone else to check it?

So much work will have gone into the various stages of building your portfolio and it is crucial you don't slip up at this point. In this chapter we will consider the structure and layout of your portfolio, the steps towards submission and what happens next.

## Portfolio checklist

It seems such a simple thing to say, but you must go back to the handbook and check that you have assembled all the required elements of your portfolio. If an element is missing or incorrectly submitted your portfolio will be returned and that may cause quite a delay in the whole process of assessment. Each qualification has a checklist:

## Certification

Application form
CV
Personal statement
Personal development plan
Letter of support
Copies of training certificates or equivalent and other relevant supporting evidence.

## Chartership

CV
Personal and professional development plan
Personal evaluative statement
Evidence of participation in a Mentor Scheme
Supporting evidence.

## Fellowship

Application form
CV
Personal statement
Supporting evidence
Letters of support from Chartered Members or senior colleagues.

## Revalidation

Application form
CV
CPD log
Personal statement
Letter of support confirming the evidence provided
Supporting evidence
Audit sheet (optional).

## Structure and presentation

You have all your required elements in front of you – in folders or files – and now you have to decide how you will put the portfolio together. The arrangement of your portfolio is for you to decide, but whatever structure you decide on must enable the assessor to find all the relevant information easily. Whatever the arrangement, you should have a cover page which gives your name, your CILIP Membership number, and the qualification for which you are applying. I would suggest the contents page should follow this. Once you start to think about the contents page it helps you to visualize the organization of the portfolio.

Many colleagues have said that when they started to think about putting their portfolio together, they went out and bought new stationery. Making the portfolio attractive is important, but not as important as giving it a logical structure – although I do admit I bought three new ring binders in a pleasant lilac shade and colourful file dividers! You may decide to follow the list of required elements and just number each document individually, or you may decide to divide the portfolio into sections. Once you have decided on the order, you will need to return to the personal statement and provide reference by number to the other parts of your portfolio.

I used a very simple structure in compiling my portfolio for Fellowship; I divided the documents into ten sections:

1 Personal statement
2 Curriculum vitae

**3**  Diary: Past President and President of CILIP
**4**  Letters of support
**5**  Examples of presentations
**6**  Examples of articles
**7**  Examples of papers given at conferences
**8**  Examples of taught modules
**9**  Examples of training materials
**10**  Other documentation.

Sections 4 to 10 had multiple documents so I numbered them using a report style, for example 4.1, 4.2, 4.3, etc. At the beginning of each of these sections I listed the contents of the section. Many other colleagues prefer just to give a running number to each document in the collection. There is no right or wrong way, so long as it is clear and makes it easy for the assessor. There are examples of submissions on the CILIP website and occasionally samples are also available at Qualification events run by the Career Development Group.

At this stage you need to decide what photocopies or extra printouts you need to make for the three copies you are required to submit. Don't ever send originals of certificates or awards, and always remember to keep one full copy for yourself.

## Final check and submission

Once you have organized your portfolio and put the cross-references in your personal statement, you should do the final check that your portfolio meets the assessment criteria. Re-read the assessment criteria and then read through the whole portfolio. There is still time to revise or edit! But remember not to lose sight of your target date for submission.

The final step before submission is to give your portfolio to your mentor or a critical friend. Your mentor will have seen most of the items previously so it should not take too long. If you are using a critical friend, give them a copy of the assessment form and the assessment criteria. Ask them to be honest. It is better to revise at this stage and avoid problems later down the line. I am sure you will have used a spell-check programme but do not rely on that for proofreading. Personally I am a dreadful proofreader as I read very quickly, so I always ask for help with this. I do believe it is so much better anyway for another person to look at your completed portfolio, if at all possible. Not only can they check spelling and grammar, they can also check for sense and completeness.

Now you are ready to send off the three copies. Most of us experience quite a pang when we let them go! If you are like me you will be riddled with doubts about whether the portfolio is good enough. Believe me, most people I have spoken to really do feel anxious – no matter which qualification they are applying for or whatever their experience. When you have invested such time and effort in the building of your portfolio you will feel nervous, especially as it may be some time before you hear back. Generally the process takes about two to six months. But hopefully the result will be a very positive outcome.

## What next?

Your portfolio will be sent to two assessors. They will use only the assessment form, with which you should now be very familiar, and will discuss their views. As a member of an Assessment Panel I know how much work goes into the assessment. Assessors look at the whole portfolio to determine whether you have met the criteria.

What happens if you hear that you have been asked to provide more information or attend an interview? Don't panic. You will be given very clear instructions about what is needed. Read those instructions carefully. Talk them through with your mentor or a critical friend.

If the initial assessors do not think the portfolio meets the assessment criteria, then your portfolio will go to a full Assessment Panel or to the Chartership Board, depending on the qualification. If your portfolio is then found unsatisfactory you will be given feedback from the Board or from the panel. Again, don't panic. You can resubmit and will be given a guide to time for resubmission and very full feedback. Discuss this with your mentor and resubmit.

However, if you have followed the guidelines in the handbooks, the advice given in this book – especially the information from the various contributors – and all the information on CILIP's website, then hopefully the outcome should be successful. So then you celebrate!

I have spoken to so many successful colleagues, whether they applied for Certification, Chartership, Fellowship or Revalidation, and we all share the pride in our success and our achievement. To belong to a professional association and to be judged by your peers as worthy of the CILIP award is a great feeling. Hopefully, the good habits you have got into as you compiled your portfolio will continue and you will truly become a reflective practitioner.

## Hints and tips

- ☛ Set a date for submission and plan your time to achieve that.
- ☛ Check you have all the required elements of your portfolio.
- ☛ Prepare a draft contents page and make sure that the portfolio is organized to help the assessors find all the information easily.
- ☛ Look at the assessment criteria again before you submit your portfolio and double-check that you have included evidence for all assessment criteria.
- ☛ Check that your evidence is cross-referenced from your personal statement.
- ☛ Get someone else to do a final proofread.
- ☛ Celebrate your success!

### CASE STUDY 8.1
**Jim Jackson: The Certification experience**

Portfolio management needs to be done in a logical and calculated manner. It has often been described as 'the one time that size does matter' (referring to the fact that quality normally takes precedence in portfolio presentation). Having previously completed four NVQs I was aware of the value of a portfolio and the Certification portfolio needs the same style of production, but in a highly condensed format. In her book *NVQs and How to Get Them*, Hazel Dakers (1996) describes a portfolio as 'not a random selection so much as a concise collection of evidence of your ability'. This is true today for the ACLIP candidate and needs to be seen as an opportunity to demonstrate skills and competencies.

## Your CV

The CV can be used to document additional tasks which there might not be room for in other parts of the portfolio. It is generally accepted that the CV needs to be in reverse chronological order of employment and qualifications, with your current post showing what position you hold. I found putting together a CV very challenging as I had not produced one for many years and wanted to expand on some of my experiences, the opportunities I had taken and, of course, my successes. This needed to be done not as an academic essay but as a brief and concise evaluation of all that I had learned. Of all the skills a library assistant learns, evaluation is the most important. Descriptive skills are, of course, important but an analysis of what you have done and what you have gained shows why you should be offered opportunities for continuing professional development. My CV shows my progression from library assistant working in a small departmental library to senior information assistant and library supervisor for a branch library. There is a progression of training, application of new skills, forward planning and professional involvement in external events and organizations. Membership of the appropriate group of CILIP cannot be overestimated as it provides valuable opportunities to participate in and contribute to activities to which you may not have access at work.

All of this can be apparent from a clear and concise portfolio, with a good CV at the front to invite the assessor to look carefully at the rest of the evidence in the portfolio. Your CV reflects your past successes while your personal development plan shows your future plans and objectives. It is important to consider the portfolio as an integrated set of items rather than separate documents, as it can demonstrate what a candidate has achieved, how they did it, what they learned from it all, and where they want it to take them. It is possible to use the CV to cross-reference to other evidence, but I found this very difficult to do. I also think it detracts from the important information that the CV is trying to convey.

## Assembling your portfolio

I think the clearest way to start putting a portfolio together is to, first, gather all your evidence documents together in one pile. Then divide them into sections on the following lines: certificates of achievement, examples of projects, evidence of completion of projects and, finally, correspondence and witness support statements. Now examine each pile with a view to looking for documents which show achievement, such as an ILS NVQ certificate listing the units completed. This can show your success in a variety of fields and therefore there is no need for extra evidence. From your projects pile select the best project from your collection to show your involvement in and the success of the project and how it has affected working practices. Don't be modest here – it's your chance to demonstrate your effectiveness in the workplace – but don't claim something you could not prove if asked to do so.

Finally, correspondence. This needs to show how your imaginative ideas and communication skills have worked over a range of projects. This could be from organizing in-house training for staff to public displays and events. With this small number of documents you have to see whether you can cover all the criteria listed in the Certification handbook. Your evidence can be used in more than one instance, provided that it shows a different aspect of the required criteria. Number your pages clearly, so that cross-referencing is possible without a lot of page turning and hunting for relevance.

You have to accept the word limit for the personal statement template, and not add an extra 10%, hoping no one will mind. Completing the forms is part of the skills of carrying out instructions as required. But it does give you a chance to list what you have achieved, perhaps without even knowing it, in terms of understanding your workplace key roles and mission.

## Life after Certification

Having achieved your Certification the first thing you can do is use the post-nominals ACLIP after your name! Your ACLIP is your demonstration of your skills and competencies, and something to be proud of. Perhaps this will inspire you to continue with your CPD and consider registering for Chartership by

CILIP. If your job offers the necessary development opportunities this is a real possibility, and one which you should seriously consider. Following my successful application for Certification, I have felt so much more confident in myself and in the work I do. I have been fortunate to be asked to speak at various training events where other potential Certification candidates wanted to know more about this scheme. I have learned more about making presentations to big and small groups and have used different types of technology, including PowerPoint via remote control and via a 'white board' – all of which I can use within my own organization if the need arises.

I would urge people to take a full and active part in their professional organization because they are its membership; they have an input into the policies and procedures. This is how we came to have the Framework of Qualifications in the first place, by membership leadership. You don't have to take on roles you are not happy with, but there is training available to you, and the committee members I have met are always keen to offer help. In 2006 I was asked whether I would take over editorship of the affiliates' web pages, something I had never done before. But I attended a training session, asked for advice and experimented with it. Our affiliates' web pages are now up and 'live' and receive regular updates. There is no such thing as 'can't' do that; there's 'can't be bothered', but you will need to take control of your own professional training to a certain extent and, if workplace opportunities are few and far between, you should use your initiative and take leave and go in your own time. It may lead you on to other qualifications, which in turn may get you that new job you always wanted but were afraid to apply for.

## CASE STUDY 8.2
### Chloe French: The Chartership experience

Compiling a portfolio of professional development is a daunting challenge and at the start of the process I, like many other Chartership candidates, felt overwhelmed by the task that lay ahead of me. I embarked on the Chartership process within a year of completing my Library and Information Studies Master's qualification. I knew the process would be very different from the academic one to which I was accustomed, but that I would need to apply the same methodical approach in order to create a successful portfolio.

One of the most important things I learned is that it takes time to develop a full understanding of the Chartership process and how to create an effective portfolio. My first step was to gather information about portfolio building, as this was an entirely new form of assessment for me. I read the Chartered Membership handbook and articles from CILIP's list of suggested reading. I collected features offering portfolio advice from the *Library and Information Gazette* and from *Impact*, the journal of CILIP's Career Development Group. I attended a Chartership advisory course where I met fellow Chartership candidates. There is a lot of information to absorb in the initial stages, but with time it all starts to make sense.

My first sense of achievement came with the submission of my personal professional development plan. This was the first time I had written such a plan, but with the help of an experienced mentor I was introduced to the concept of self-directed learning. I learned valuable strategies for identifying and expressing my training and development needs. My Chartership journey became much clearer once I had identified these needs, established how I would meet them and what I would learn on the way. At this stage I decided that the aim of my portfolio would be to demonstrate my development in the early stages of my professional career.

## Gathering the evidence

With these clear goals established I then focused on undertaking the training identified in my development plan and gaining experience in my everyday job. Initially I gathered pieces of evidence demonstrating my development from all areas of my work. There was no form of selection at this stage. I wanted to collect as much as I could, so that I would be able to choose the most suitable examples to enter into the final portfolio. For example, I kept a log of training events I attended, certificates of attendance, meeting agendas and minutes, as well as examples of my everyday work. Yet I still felt uneasy about how I would present this evidence in my portfolio. Again, it took time for me to work out the best ways to present all the information I had gathered.

I reviewed my ever-increasing collection of evidence at regular intervals – often in preparation for a meeting with my mentor. These meetings provided the opportunity to reflect on the progress I was making. Each time we met, my understanding of the Chartership process improved, as did my confidence in my portfolio-building skills.

## Preparing the portfolio

About ten months into the Chartership process I began to contemplate how I would build my portfolio. At this point I decided to consult a couple of examples of successful submissions to see different ways of organizing all the necessary documentation. I found this both encouraging and a little unsettling, because they were very different from what I was preparing, but it was important to remember that a portfolio is a very personal document and that each candidate will approach the task in their own distinctive way.

Once I had completed the actions in my development plan it was time to commit to compiling the portfolio. I set about this in the way I had always done with academic exercises, simply because I knew this worked for me. I re-read all the information supplied by CILIP to ensure I understood the assessment criteria and then I wrote out the criteria and stuck them on the wall in front of my desk. This would ensure that everything I included in the portfolio related to the assessment criteria and that I was always writing reflectively – analysing my performance and considering the impact of training events on my professional development.

I chose to divide my evaluative statement, and consequently the pieces of evidence, into four sections based on the assessment criteria. In the first section I introduced myself and presented my development plan. In the second I analysed my personal performance, focusing on the core areas of my professional development. In the third, I evaluated the performance of the library service for which I work. In the final section I displayed my commitment to continuing professional development by reflecting on developmental events I had attended and by providing details of my professional reading and the ways I had used this within my job.

Writing the evaluative statement requires discipline in order to present the relevant information within the word limit. I chose to offer brief initial analysis in the personal statement with an immediate reference to the relevant piece of evidence in the appendices section. The evidence section of the portfolio was my opportunity to elaborate on my professional development. My aim was to present a clear picture to an assessor who might have very little knowledge of my sector. As well as remembering to address the relevant assessment criteria, I also knew that I had to make the report easy and inviting to read. Consequently, I wanted to present my evidence in a variety of formats. For example, I chose to present some training events in a table so that it was clear to see at a glance the courses I had attended, what I had learned and how I would apply this new knowledge to my job. For other courses I included a certificate of attendance and a piece of reflective writing highlighting what I had gained from the experience.

## Conclusion

Compiling a portfolio of professional development marked my transition from an academic to a professional style of writing and presenting information. I used the writing and analytical skills I had developed at university, but this time I was applying them to myself. Building my portfolio has equipped me with the skills to analyse my strengths and weaknesses and take control of my own learning and development. I have become more self-aware and have developed the habit of not just acquiring new skills, but reflecting on how these improve my ability to perform my job. Taking responsibility for your own learning and development is a challenge, but also an essential workplace skill. Chartership and creating a portfolio were demanding tasks, but critically analysing your own performance is rarely easy. The time and effort I put into the creation of my portfolio resulted in a document of which I am proud and, more importantly, has developed in me a set of skills which will prove invaluable throughout my career.

CASE STUDY 8.3
**Atiya Afghan: From ACLIP to MCLIP, the Chartership Experience**

Putting together a portfolio wasn't as daunting for me as it could be for those who were applying for Chartership via a conventional pathway. I was fortunate in a sense to have taken the alternative route offered by CILIP for those who find themselves working in a library and starting with little or, in my case, no knowledge of librarianship. I came to into the profession (by accident and good fortune!) in September 2004 and reached the dizzy heights of Chartered Status by May 2009!

## Learning from experience

I say that it was not as difficult only because my previous two qualifications, NVQ level 3 in Library and Information Management and ACLIP, both required me to present a portfolio. Therefore, by the time I had decided to aim for Chartership I was building on previous experience. I had realized the value and importance of being a qualified librarian, so I worked from NVQ to Chartership without pausing for breath. This was because I enjoyed learning and the more I learned the more I realized how much more there was to learn!

The NVQ required me to demonstrate my awareness as a librarian of basic knowledge such as the Dewey Decimal Classification (DDC) and producing an effective display. The ACLIP required me to start thinking, planning and putting into action my plans and looking at the outcomes, but with the Chartership I was required to take my work to a higher, more professional level; it required me to think, plan, put into action, evaluate then re-plan and then start the cycle again, confirming that learning is an ongoing and active process. I discovered later that this cycle is known as *experiential learning* based on *Kolb's experiential learning theory* model.

## Starting Chartership

While I was awaiting my results for the ACLIP application, I was promoted to Head Librarian. As soon as my ACLIP status was awarded, I wasted no time in contacting my mentor to arrange a meeting to discuss my progression towards Chartership – after all, this was my goal. The next step was to download the Chartership handbook and read the guidelines thoroughly. I found that it was necessary to read this guide regularly over the next two years in order to keep in mind the *assessment criteria* and stay focused.

My meetings with my mentor played a huge part in the Chartership process. Once Sarah Pavey had agreed to continue mentoring me (Sarah had seen me through both the NVQ and ACLIP), we discussed what my aims were for the library, what I wanted to include in my *personal professional development plan* (PPDP) and how long I thought I would need to document evidence before submission. I liked working to a deadline as I found that it stopped me from getting distracted and helped me to stay resolute. We agreed that mid-2009 would give me sufficient time, and that was back in spring 2007. It is very important to log your meetings with your mentor; it doesn't have to be detailed but should include the date of your meetings and the essence of what was discussed as you are required to produce a *mentor log* in your portfolio.

## The PPDP

The PPDP required some thought, and by looking at the handbook I realized that it included useful guidance. I was required to become familiar with my organization and its structure (you will also need to produce an *organizational structure chart*) and its aims and objectives, and understand my place within it. This meant that I had to examine closely my position within the school and how I could work to benefit its overall aims. As I found that I was now managing a team and had no previous experience, I searched and found relevant training for the new role. By doing this, I was demonstrating that I was able to *analyse personal and professional development* just as the assessment criteria required me to do.

The PPDP is not set in stone; it's natural to change and adapt it as your situations alter. It's a good idea to record the changes regularly and discuss them with your mentor. It is also essential that you become involved in the profession and attend at least one CPD session – you will be asked for evidence of this, so ensure that you come away with a certificate of attendance for every event or training session that you attend. In addition, make sure you write a brief account of any training, as well as what you gained from it and how you will use it in your setting. At a later stage, go back and evaluate what you did and decide if it could be improved. This demonstrates *critical reflection* on your personal performance and also provides evidence that you *evaluate your service performance*, both of which are essential requirements of the Chartership.

## Collecting evidence

My change in role meant that I didn't have to think too hard of things to include in my portfolio. I knew that I would have to learn new skills and that I would be making changes to develop the library in line with the school development plan. Each time I changed something or made any improvements I recorded it and collected photographic evidence to support my claim. I collected evidence indiscriminately at first, and when I finally got nearer to putting the portfolio together I selected the best examples of my work. This isn't as easy as it sounds and it is very tempting to put in too much; it was good to have Sarah's guidance at this point and I finally put the temptation behind me. I used a variety of ways to show the assessors how much I had learned and put into practice. I used written evidence, plenty of pictures and digital evidence on a CD-ROM as well as a USB stick. I also asked for letters of support from users of the library. I approached everyone from the Headmaster to my assistants, including students and even parents, as my initiatives extended to the wider community of the School. Sarah had advised me to make the portfolio as interesting as possible by making it 'tell a story'; I tried to do just that.

I became actively involved in the profession by joining a special interest group, the School Librarian's Group National, when I was invited to do so. I also joined two other local school librarians' groups and organized training sessions for local librarians. This increased my skills and knowledge about my profession as it offered me the opportunity to meet with some high profile librarians to discuss the profession and issues that we had in common. I also jumped at any other opportunities whenever they arose, such as giving a talk or writing about the ACLIP experience for librarians who were considering professional qualifications.

Finally, I took it upon myself to visit other libraries at universities to get a better understanding of the profession at different levels. I visited Oxford

(Bodleian), Cambridge, Imperial, London School of Economics and The School of Oriental and African Studies and a variety of other public and school libraries. I wanted to see what was offered to the students when they got there. I managed to take away some ideas and adapt them for the students at my school, for example the use of USB sticks as part of the 6th form inductions (an idea I saw being used at the Law Library at Oxford). This showed I was aware of the broader picture of the information profession and that I was able to evaluate ideas I saw there thus fulfilling another important part of the assessment criteria *breadth of professional knowledge and understanding of the wider profession.*

## Conclusion

The whole experience was demanding but exhilarating. It helped me to understand the significance of experiential learning and how it could contribute to my becoming a professional librarian. But most of all I learnt that taking a proactive approach to the Chartership not only produced a higher standard of work, but made it easier to compile the portfolio. The process of Chartership has helped me both professionally, by opening new doors, and personally, by increasing my confidence and furthering my desire to learn. My next goal is to aim for the Fellowship, and in the meanwhile, complete a BA in Humanities with the Open University.

## CASE STUDY 8.4
**Shamin Renwick: The Fellowship experience**

> The difference between a job and a career is the difference between forty and sixty hours a week.
>
> (Robert Frost)

Thanks to the ubiquitous nature of information technology today, those hours could be increased and need not be restricted to a desk at the office. My appreciation and commitment to the profession has been my driving force as I truly enjoy being a librarian.

Having had the pleasure and opportunity to serve at the executive level of our national association as well as at the highest level in the regional library association (as President of the Association of Caribbean University, Research and Institutional Libraries [ACURIL] in 2003–4), I wanted to be involved in the profession at an international level. Coming from a developing society, getting involved in the Chartered Institute of Library and Information Professionals in the UK, as well as others, such as the American Library Association (ALA) and the International Federation of Library Associations and Institutions (IFLA), would be a natural expansion to gain experience and keep up to date with professional activities at an advanced level, which should in turn impact on my work in the region.

Dr Alma Jordan MCLIP, former University Librarian at University of the West Indies and a long-standing Member of The Library Association, was instrumental in my getting involved in CILIP. In keeping abreast of CILIP's activities through its comprehensive and well structured website, I noted the criteria for becoming a Fellow and felt that if my application was successful, there would only be positive outcomes.

Being unable to access any of the substantial preparation, training and mentorship provided to Members living in the UK, I decided to adhere closely to the application guidelines, which I studied in detail (translate: read, re-read and summarized). Little else about the process was available on the internet. I must say 'thanks' to the members of the Qualifications and Professional Development Department for managing the process efficiently.

The practice of maintaining a detailed CV over the years proved worthwhile, as this comprehensive record served well to recall activities and achievements accomplished early in my career.

Several prominent librarians (local and regional) with whom I had collaborated over the years enthusiastically provided letters of support. Though great achievers themselves, only one was a Fellow of CILIP (FCLIP), so an explanation of application procedures and the criteria to be satisfied was necessary. I also shared information about CILIP and, as the name is relatively new, explained its origins in the LA (a name with which most people were familiar).

## Personal statement

Writing a personal statement in 500 words was indeed quite a challenge, as it would be for all persons applying for Fellowship. It was written in three parts, matching the three areas in which a Fellow had to have substantial achievement, namely professional practice, contribution to all or part of the profession and active commitment to professional development. I am grateful for comments and advice from Professor Derek Law, whom I asked to review my application.

An extremely useful task was preparing a carefully formatted document in which the personal statement was rewritten, and, for each point made, the relevant items of evidence were inserted. Typical of the stereotyped librarian who keeps everything, I had actually retained some documents (in pre-electronic typeface) over the years, unsure of whether they would ever be useful except for some nostalgic reason. They took me back to a time and place in my career where the possibility of acquiring the most prestigious qualification in the profession would not have occurred to me.

## Gathering and presenting evidence

Gathering and selecting evidence, like the personal statement, required a great deal of thought and planning, Items of evidence could take different formats. The result of the work of committees, not just a list of committees, would be more meaningful. Letters from notable persons can support a perspective on an accomplishment; for example, a letter of commendation or congratulations for receiving an award instead of just a list of achievements can be submitted. Evidence could be an item at different periods of time; for example, an annual report written early in your career and one many years later could illustrate growth, both in ability to communicate as well as in duties undertaken and how you executed them as your career grew. Depending on the activity or point being presented, e-mail threads can provide an excellent record.

A great deal of attention was paid to the presentation of the entire portfolio, ensuring that the formatting and organization made it uncomplicated to review. For easy reference, each item of evidence had a cover page with a statement of what it was, why it was selected, and a numbering system which linked it to the list of evidence. Double-checking for errors was essential, as this submission was a reflection of me and I would be judged on both content and presentation.

## Reflections on achieving Fellowship

Some of the benefits of being elected to the register of Fellows are universal. Undoubtedly it brings tremendous prestige to one's name and reputation and, by association, to one's employer and other affiliations. Post-nominal letters are impressive and give professional authority to one's name. No one can deny the value in the world of academia where post-nominals, placed on business cards and next to signatures, are the standard by which achievements are recognized and celebrated, carrying a weight of authority and expertise. And in the case of the FCLIP, which is by no means a commonplace qualification even in the UK, this honour is greatly valued.

Recognition of one's achievements and commitment by the wider society, as sought through Fellowship, is welcome and necessary. It is a great motivation for the person being acknowledged to continue striving to perform at an even higher level, and underlines that service is not in vain. Many national library associations in the Caribbean suffer, as do other small associations around the world, from a lack of critical mass of members to make them work efficiently and, in the case of the regional association, ACURIL (Association of Caribbean University, Research and Institutional Libraries), the membership is separated by water, distance, language and culture. Flagging attendance and a lack of support for activities are endemic. It is my fervent hope that this achievement of the highest professional qualification can be seen as a reward and a much-needed incentive to inspire colleagues who feel similarly about commitment to the profession and to continuing education, as well as volunteer service, as they seek the betterment of both themselves and their organizations.

Acknowledgement is necessary and Fellowship is one way to gain this. I also hope that it can be seen as a tangible goal to work towards for colleagues who may no longer be striving for academic achievement but wish to contribute to professional practice in a meaningful way.

The opportunity for self-reflection was greatly valued. The thought process involved in self-appraisal, which probably would not be done under other circumstances, was most beneficial and appreciated. No other task undertaken over the years called for this degree of introspection and self-evaluation. Having to analyse, admit to oneself, document and justify to others one's thoughts about oneself was a revealing exercise.

Over the years, you work dedicatedly, often moving from project to project, occasionally wondering why, and sometimes feeling unappreciated. My career has taken several unexpected turns, challenges have been many and, as experienced by us all at some time or other, there has been unavoidable professional jealousy; factors which can deter from working towards laudable goals. So attaining Fellowship status has provided a much-needed justification, especially when time is taken from family, as vacations are all working ones and stress levels are generally high. It has engendered a sense of overcoming obstacles and that maintaining my planned course was worthwhile.

The honour bestowed by being granted the highest professional qualification from an esteemed institution like the Chartered Institute gave me a sense of personal fulfilment unrivalled by other achievements to date. It was a major highlight in my career so far and, I am sure, will number among the most valued at the end of it.

The experience of preparing the portfolio has enhanced my skills in self-assessment as well as in the assessment of others, acquiring managerial skills important in human resource tasks, such as the selection and recruitment of staff. It provided processes and procedures which can be utilized for other projects requiring analysis and documentation. It has enhanced my standing in the profession, recognizing my seniority, and provides authority for my position as a mentor.

Having to reflect on and analyse the path of my career, taking note of changes in direction and why I had made the choices I did, how much I had achieved and where my support came from, was invaluable in taking stock of my entire life thus far. It has prepared me to go on to another level of existence – a new phase of my career and life, opening up a whole new world.

CASE STUDY 8.5
## Michael Martin: The Revalidation experience

Two years after CILIP's Framework of Qualifications was introduced, I sent in my portfolio to revalidate my Chartership. I had conflicting feelings about starting the process. On the one hand my professional body was offering recognition for the learning and development I had undertaken over the last decade, creating a vital means of personal development to deliver a powerful message to employers and clients that our profession takes development seriously. On the other hand, it was extra work that Chartered Members of CILIP had managed without for more than a century.

However, I could not ignore it. Even though there's no obligation for Chartered Members to revalidate, I was deeply implicated in CILIP's Framework of Qualifications. I had observed the meetings where the qualification was developed, I work for the Institute that promotes the award and I'd been extolling the benefits of portfolio building at meetings, courses and conferences all around the country for more than two years. Also I had been Chartered for ten years, so could revalidate immediately. I had no excuse, so the time had come to put my money where my mouth was. To be fair, it was only £22 and my mouth had been doing a lot of work.

For this case study I went back to the first draft of my statement. Reading it several months further on, I see that I fell into the trap of describing and not evaluating and of not making the most of my evidence.

## Make the most of your evidence

I'll give an example: one of the pieces of evidence I thought about using was an article by Bob McKee (2006). Bob's article in a recent *Update* highlighted 'six good reasons' for joining CILIP. Part of my responsibilities at CILIP is to encourage student Membership. This succinct argument has proved useful for the so-called 'lift conversation' where you tell someone about your job or, in this case, about your organization, before the end of the 'lift journey'.

In the final draft this didn't survive because there were two problems.

The first problem was that, although it was useful, it was not very substantial. I did not have material evidence showing that anybody had joined or retained Membership of CILIP as a result of using it. I could have said that I felt more confident in speaking to groups with this reading behind me, and that it would help me do my job better. But there were other events which were more demonstrably useful.

The second problem was that the main piece of evidence was an article written by somebody else. I could have just included an abstract, but the credit still goes somewhere else. All it said about me was that I did the reading. An assessor might conclude that I was able to act upon it and derive benefit for my Institute, thereby just about meeting the third criterion – 'Evidence of continuous professional development through reading, participation in professional affairs and contribution to or attendance at courses/conference, etc.' There were only three criteria to meet; I should be able to find better evidence that said more about me.

For the final draft I believe I had two major improvements, and both came from the same exercise. By completing the CPD audit, which is available on the CILIP website, I found far better evidence to draw upon, and by adding the audit to the portfolio I was, intrinsically, including evaluation in the portfolio.

In the following paragraph I referred to a flowchart I had included in a leaflet designed to introduce the CILIP Framework of Qualifications:

> Having worked with consultants putting together a database for the new
> framework I can now write specifications and have learned how to use flowcharts
> to clarify processes. I used this in the leaflet I wrote introducing CILIP's
> Framework of Qualifications (flowchart in Item 3).

In the explanatory paragraph to the leaflet, I described how consultants for another project used flowcharts to help them understand our work and how they explained that the flowchart has to be a simple diagram describing only one process. I used this method in my leaflet, which was praised for clarity. Looking back on this now, I can see that I did not make it clear that I had written and worked in collaboration with a designer on the leaflet. Don't make the same mistake – exploit the evidence as fully as you can.

## My goals in revalidating

As well as revalidating my Chartership and adding value to my own professional development, I had three other goals:

1 I wanted to prove that a portfolio need not be huge. We tell candidates that they must not overload their Chartership and Certification portfolios. Meet the criteria and then stop. This shows good judgement and confidence in the material. Easier said than done. When you are the candidate you are tempted to overwhelm the assessor with all your knowledge, achievements and learning.
2 I wanted to demonstrate that for a Revalidation candidate assembling a portfolio need not be a huge task, it should complement their job. Without a specified deadline, and being an award which brings no easily measurable benefit (financial or visible recognition), candidates must feel that Revalidation is achievable and worthwhile.
3 I wanted to identify key advice that could easily be passed on to other candidates for the whole Framework of Qualifications.

I believe I was successful in these aims:

1 My portfolio was 23 pages long, including the two A4 sides of the statement, the audit and the training log. I could probably have been bolder and made it even smaller.
2 Without the procrastination, I think I put in about eight hours' work in total. I have a tendency to underestimate the time tasks take; however, I do not believe assembling the portfolio impinged greatly on my family life.
3 If I were to pass on one hint to future Revalidation candidates it would be to do the CPD audit first. It will save you time and effort in the long run by helping you find good evidence and identify the training and development that has meant the most to you.

## Some reflections on Revalidation

Revalidation sometimes leads to an increase in salary, not always or often, but it does help you do your work better, which may put you in line for an increment. It may not be a requirement in a job advert, but having put together a portfolio you are in the frame of mind that thinks about achievements and outcomes, which is ideal for job applications.

What Revalidation does is help you to assess your training and recognize what has contributed to your development. The process of writing, collecting and reflecting adds value to the training and experience you already have. Even writing this case study has prompted me to reflect on the benefits of Revalidating and consider how I could do it better.

Reflection is stopping and taking the time to learn from achievements and mistakes so that you can make decisions about your future, and any exercise which makes you do this is personally valuable.

I was informed that my application had been successful in June 2007. At first it was a huge relief, then a source of pride. I do not believe Revalidation should be compulsory; it is an award that should prove its value. However, I do think a visible recognition in the form of post-nominals would make the award more attractive.

# Bibliography

Booth, A. and Brice, A. (eds) (2004) *Evidence-based Practice for Information Professionals: a handbook*, Facet Publishing.

Boud, D., Keogh, R. and Walker, D. (1985) *Reflection: turning experience into learning*, Kogan Page.

Boydell, T. and Leary, M. (1986) *Identifying Training Needs*, Institute of Personnel and Development.

Brine, A. (2005) *Continuing Professional Development: a guide for information professionals*, Chandos Publishing.

Brine, A. and Feather, J. (2003) Building a Skills Portfolio for the Information Professional, *New Library World*, **104** [1194/1195], 455–63.

Cameron, J. (1997) *The Vein of Gold: a journey to your creative heart*, Pan Books.

Chapman, J. (1991) *Journaling for Joy: writing your way to personal growth and freedom*, Newcastle Publishing.

CIPFA (n.d.) *Initial Professional Development Scheme: reflective writing*, www.cipfa.org.uk/students/current/download/IPDS_Reflective_ writing_booklet.pdf.

Dakers, H. (1996) *NVQs and How to Get Them*, Kogan Page.

Gibbons, A. *CPD and Lifelong Learning*, www.andrewgibbons.co.uk/cpd.html.

Hall, F. and Barker, C. (2005) Producing a Portfolio, *Impact*, **8** (4), 81–2.

Herzog, J. (1996) *Implementing S/NVQs in the Information and Library Sector: a guide for employers*, Library Association Publishing.

Honey, P. and Mumford, A. (1986) *The Manual of Learning Styles*, Peter Honey Publications.

Honey, P. and Mumford, A. (2000) *The Learning Styles Helper's Guide*, Peter Honey Publications.

Hood, I. (2006) Practical Portfolio Tips, *Library and Information Gazette*, 2 June.

Jackson, N. (2001) *Personal Development Planning: what does it mean?* PDP Working Paper 1, LTSN (Learning and Teaching Subject Network) Generic Centre.

Klauser, H. A. (1986) *Writing on Both Sides of the Brain: breakthrough techniques for people who write*, Harper & Row.

Kolb, D. (1986) *Experiential Learning: experience as the source of learning and development*, Prentice Hall.

Marshall, K. (2006) The Chartership Process and Planning for Continuing Professional Development, *Impact*, **9** (1), 4–5.

McKee, B. (2006) Sustaining CILIP: some questions answered, *Library & Information Update*, April, 5 (4), 20–1.

Raddon, R. (ed.) (2005) *Your Career, Your Life: career management for the information professional*, Ashgate.

Rolfe, G., Freshwater, D. and Jasper, M. (2001) *Critical Reflection for Nursing and the Helping Professions: a user's guide*, Palgrave.

Thomson, B. (2006) *Growing People: learning and developing from day to day experience*, Chandos Publishing.

Watton, P., Collings, J. and Moon, J. (n.d.) *Reflective Writing: guidance notes for students*, www.ex.ac.uk/employability/students/reflective.rtf.

Watts, A. W. (1957) *The way of Zen*, Penguin.

Webb, S. and Grimwood-Jones, D. (2003) *Personal Development in the Information and Library Profession*, 3rd edn, Europa Publications.

Williamson, M. (1986) *Training Needs Analysis*, Library Association Publishing.

## Websites

Andrew Gibbons' website, www.andrewgibbons.co.uk.

CILIP: Body of Professional Knowledge,
www.cilip.org.uk/jobs-careers/qualifications/accreditation/bpk/Pages/default.aspx.

CILIP Qualifications,
www.cilip.org.uk/jobs-careers/qualifications/cilip-qualifications/Pages/default.aspx.

Recording Skills Development for Information and Library Skills Portfolio,
www.ics.heacademy.ac.uk/resources/links/is_skills.php.

Michael Martin's qualifications blog,
http://communities.cilip.org.uk/blogs/quals/default.aspx.

TFPL's Knowledge and Information Skills Toolkit,
www.tfpl.com/skills_development/skills_competencies.cfm#stk.

# Index